HORRIBLE SCIENCE

DANGER

NASTY NATURE

Nick Arnold Illustrated by **Tony De Saulles**

■SCHOLASTIC

www.horrible-science.co.uk

Scholastic Children's Books,
Euston House, 24 Eversholt Street,
London NW1 1DB, UK

A division of Scholastic Ltd
London ~ New York ~ Toronto ~ Sydney ~ Auckland
Mexico City ~ New Delhi ~ Hong Kong

First published in the UK by Scholastic Ltd, 1996
Abridged edition first published by Scholastic Ltd, 2014
This edition published 2018

Text © Nick Arnold, 1997, 2014, 2018
Illustrations © Tony De Saulles, 1997, 2014
Index by Caroline Hamilton

ISBN 978 1407 18539 2

Printed and bound by CPI Group (UK) Ltd, Croydon, CR0 4YY

2 4 6 8 10 9 7 5 3 1

The right of Nick Arnold and Tony De Saulles to be identified as the author
and illustrator of this work respectively has been asserted by them in accordance
with the Copyright, Designs and Patents Act, 1988.

CONTENTS

Nick Arnold has been writing stories and books since he was a youngster, but never dreamt he'd find fame writing about Nasty Nature. His research involved grappling with lions, talking to dumb animals and cuddling up to snakes and he enjoyed every minute of it.

When he's not delving into Horrible Science, he spends his spare time eating pizza, riding his bike and thinking up corny jokes (though not all at the same time).

www.nickarnold-website.com

Tony De Saulles picked up his crayons when he was still in nappies and has been doodling ever since. He takes Horrible Science very seriously and even agreed to meet some of our beastly beasts before drawing them. Fortunately, he has made a full recovery.

When he's not out with his sketchpad, Tony likes to write poetry and play squash, though he hasn't written any poetry about squash yet.

www.tonydesaulles.co.uk

INTRODUCTION

Brute force. Beastly behaviour. Animal cunning. Whenever humans have anything nasty to say to one another they drag animals into it. And animals bring out the worst in some humans, which can lead to nasty situations…

The science of animals can also provide some nasty surprises (and we're not talking about your brutish, wolfish, slavering teacher here). What, for example, about the odd words scientists use to describe our four-legged friends? They certainly leave a nasty taste in your mouth – when you don't understand them.

*ENGLISH TRANSLATION: COR – WHAT A NICE MOGGIE!

This is rather a pity because it's the nasty side of animals that gives them their horrible fascination. Obviously, we're not talking warm and cuddly here. You might be pleased to wake up and find a fluffy kitten or a playful puppy on your bed. But what about a giant green toad with staring eyes and warty skin? Or a sociable skunk, or even a grinning gila monster with huge claws?

Yep. Some creatures are cold and slimy with gigantic teeth. Others like to suck blood and live in horrible places. In a word – they're NASTY. And oddly enough that's what this book is about. Nasty Nature. The sort of things that 99 per cent of teachers wouldn't dream of teaching in their worst nightmares.

But who knows? After you've read up on reptiles and mugged up on mammals you could persuade your teacher that you're a 'natural' scientist. Perhaps you might even discover a new kind of nasty creature. Or feel inspired to keep a new pet…

One thing's for sure. Science will never seem the same again!

FREAKY CREATURES

Sometimes it takes a difficult person to crack a really difficult problem. And 300 years ago, scientists had an appallingly difficult problem. Explorers kept discovering freaky new kinds of animals – but how should scientists go about listing this huge variety of new creatures? It was a toughie.

Hall of fame: Carl Linnaeus (1707–1778)
Nationality: Swedish

Carl Linnaeus was a difficult man. It wasn't simply that he was an inspired genius with an incredible memory. The trouble was that he knew he was, and he wanted everyone else to know, too. If anyone criticized him he turned nasty. He sulked like a spoilt child and he never admitted he was wrong – never, ever, ever. Not even when he made big mistakes, like claiming a hippopotamus was a kind of rat!

HIPPOPOTAMUS

BLIMEY – MY CAT CAUGHT ONE OF THOSE LAST NIGHT!

To be fair to Carl he'd seen rats before but not hippos.

But when Carl gave lectures, hundreds of students flocked to hear him. Why? Because he also told jokes. (A scientist with a sense of humour – now there's a rarity.)

9

CARL'S QUEST

Carl Linnaeus had itchy feet – that's to say he never stopped moving around … and working. He travelled 7,499 km across northern Scandinavia and discovered 100 plants that were unknown to science. But his main aim was far more ambitious. This was to sort out all the plants and all the animals in the world into some kind of logical order.

Unfortunately, he liked some animals more than others. He had particularly nasty things to say about amphibia – that's creatures such as frogs and toads that live on land and in water…

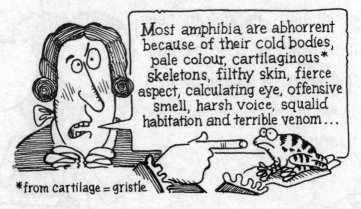

Most amphibia are abhorrent because of their cold bodies, pale colour, cartilaginous* skeletons, filthy skin, fierce aspect, calculating eye, offensive smell, harsh voice, squalid habitation and terrible venom…

*from cartilage = gristle

Carl had his work cut out. There's an enormous variety of animals in the world. And thousands more were being discovered every year in unlikely places.

BET YOU NEVER KNEW!
There are currently about 10,000,000,000,000,000, 000,000,000,000,000,000 (that's 10 billion, trillion, trillion) animals on Earth (give or take a few million) and they come in all shapes and sizes.

NOT A BAD SORT...

So how did Linnaeus sort 'em all out? He said that every type of animal was a species. Take this rather ugly toad.

NO THANKS

Following Linnaeus' plan, scientists call the toad a *Bufo bufo* – *bufo* is the name of the species and *Bufo* is the name of the genus it belongs to. (A genus is a group of similar species.) In fact, Bufo means 'toad' in Latin, so the scientific name actually means 'Toad toad'.

Linnaeus placed each genus into a larger category called a family and grouped the families into classes. (Nothing to do with school you'll be relieved to know!) Our toad belongs to the family *Bufonidae* (Boo-fo-nid-ay) which includes toads and frogs, and the class Amphibia which also includes their slimy relatives, the salamanders and newts.

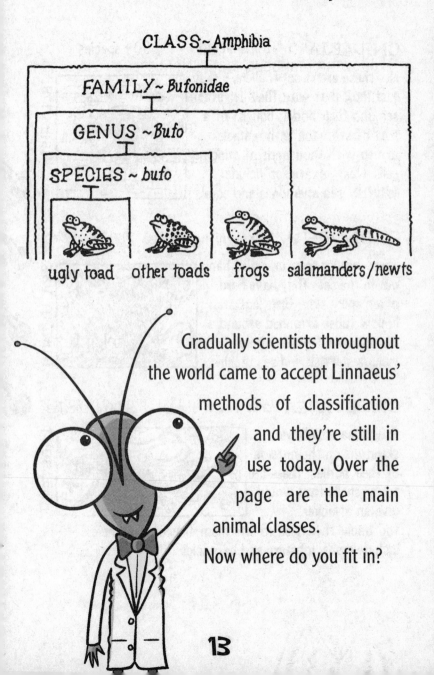

CLASS ~ Amphibia

FAMILY ~ Bufonidae

GENUS ~ Bufo

SPECIES ~ bufo

ugly toad   other toads   frogs   salamanders/newts

Gradually scientists throughout the world came to accept Linnaeus' methods of classification and they're still in use today. Over the page are the main animal classes.

Now where do you fit in?

CNIDARIA (ni-dare-ee-uh) - 11,000+ species

No, these aren't sci-fi aliens – they just look that way. They live in the sea and their bodies consist of a sort of stomach with tentacles armed with thousands of stinging cells. Nasty examples include jellyfish, sea anemones and corals.

ECHINODERMS (eck-hi-no-derms) - 7,000+ species

These freaky creatures also hang out in the sea. They have hard, often spiky skin. Their legs are hollow tubes arranged around a central area. Eerie examples include starfish and sea urchins.

CRUSTACEA (crus-taysh-she-a) - 52,000+ species

Crustacea also have skeletons on the outside of their bodies. These are tough shells that would give an attacker

toothache if it tried to bite them. Crunchy examples include crabs, lobsters and barnacles.

ARACHNIDS *(arack-nids)* - 73,000 + species

The bad news: most of this class are spiders. Erk! The worse news: some are scorpions. Arachnids have their head and thorax (the middle bits) of their bodies joined together. Scorpions have a nasty poisonous sting in their tails but that doesn't stop people in Thailand enjoying roast scorpion. They have 6-12 eyes, eight jointed legs, two pincers and two grasping claws – oh, and I nearly forgot –a nasty poisonous sting in their tails. Some like playing sneaky tricks on humans – like hiding in their shoes!

FISH - 28,000+ species

Most fish have bony skeletons – so when you eat one you can end up with a face full of bones. Other fish such as sharks have gristly skeletons instead. Fish live in water (surprise, surprise) and take dissolved air from the water through the gills in the side of their heads. Most fish are covered in scales and use fins to swim. Well, they're better than arm bands.

AMPHIBIA - 6,000+ species

Amphibia are cold-blooded. That doesn't mean that they're pitiless and ruthless killers, although many are. No, 'cold-blooded' means they heat up and cool down with their surroundings. They have four legs and their skin is thin and slimy. The name amphibia means "double-lives" in Greek. And frogs and toads do live a double-life.

15

Dr Frog and Mr Tadpole

1 The tadpole hatches from eggs and gobbles up its unlucky brothers and sisters.

2 But in a few weeks it develops into a very different looking but equally repulsive adult.

3 The adult frog doesn't eat its own kind but it does grab flies with its long, sticky tongue.

4 Most amphibia spend the winter buried in mud at the bottom of lakes and ponds.

REPTILES – 8,200+ species

Reptiles are cold-blooded too, and covered in scales. They have small brains for their size and their legs stick out of the sides of their bodies so they have to crawl around. (Unless they're snakes, which slither about instead.) Young reptiles are hatched from eggs. (Don't try eating them for breakfast though.)

CHAMELEON

TORTOISE

LICK!

PLOD

PLOD

BIRDS – 10,000+ species

Birds have two legs, a pair of wings and a horny beak. (Bet you bought this book to find that out!) Their bodies are covered with feathers made from keratin – that's the same stuff as your fingernails. Young birds hatch from eggs laid by their mums. That's if the eggs don't get poached and guzzled for breakfast first.

WOODPECKER COCKEREL DUCK

PECK
PECK
PECK

COCKADOODLE-DOO

QUACK

QUACK

17

MAMMALS – 5,400 species

Mammals are warm-blooded* and most of them live on land and can't fly. Baby mammals are born alive rather than as eggs and they are nourished on milk supplied by their mums. And guess what – we're mammals too. Yes, humans belong to this class.

*This means that their blood is kept warm because their body is covered with fur or fat to keep the cold out. It's not the same as being 'hot-blooded' – that's when someone keeps losing their temper and getting into fights.

NASTY HABITATS

Animals are found everywhere you can imagine and a few places that you wouldn't want to. By the way, scientists call the place where an animal lives its 'habitat'. Animal habitats range from deserts and rainforests to coral reefs and stinking swamps.

Mountain yaks happily explore the Himalayan mountains of Tibet at heights above 5,486 metres. And they find the freezing temperatures of -17°C

(1.4°F) well, rather bracing actually. Red bears are said to climb even higher and that's how they get mistaken for the legendary yeti.

Animals also lurk in the depths of the oceans. When explorers Dr Jacques Piccard and Lt Don Walsh reached the deepest part of the ocean – 10,911 metres – in 1960, the first thing they saw was … a fish. As Piccard said later:

Slowly, very slowly, this fish moved away from us, swimming half in the bottom ooze and disappeared into the black night, the eternal night which is its domain.

The explorers were gob-smacked. They thought the weight of water crushing down on the sea floor would squash any creature.

LITTLE AND LARGE FACTS

The largest animal that has ever lived is the blue whale. This creature can grow to 33 metres long and weigh 80 tonnes. That's 24 times the size of an elephant and even bigger than the biggest dinosaur. Inside the blue whale there are over 8,500 litres of blood protected by a layer of fat 61 cm thick. But here's a nasty thought: since 1900 human hunters have brought at least 378,000 of these stupendous creatures to a horrible end.

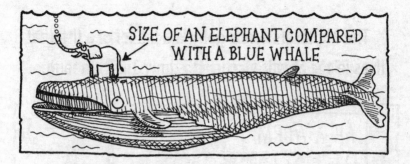

SIZE OF AN ELEPHANT COMPARED WITH A BLUE WHALE

Compare that with … Helena's hummingbird. It's only 5.7 cm from bill to tail and weighs a mere 2 grams. This tiny scrap of a creature lives off sweet, sticky nectar from flowers.

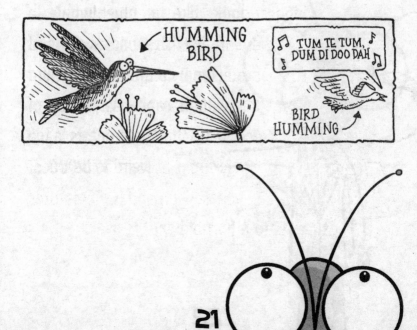

HUMMING BIRD

TUM TE TUM, DUM DI DOO DAH

BIRD HUMMING

21

The Marshall Islands goby is a tiddler of a fish that lives in the Pacific Ocean. It is only 1.27 cm long.

AH! A WORM!

← ACTUAL SIZE

But there are some creatures that make a goby fish look like a blue whale... A tiny fish sounds weird. But some creatures are Weird with a capital W. Which of these beasts is too weird to be true?

WEIRD WILDLIFE QUIZ

1 The storsjoodjuret is an ugly looking long-necked reptile that skulks around in Lake Storsjön in Sweden. It's between 10–20 metres long. TRUE/FALSE

2 There's a type of bird with a horn on its head like a unicorn. It's called a "horned screamer". TRUE/FALSE

3 The Jack Dempsey fish is named after a famous American boxer. This small South American freshwater fish got its name because it enjoys ramming into other fish and stealing their eggs. TRUE/FALSE

4 There's a type of snake that can fly short distances. TRUE/FALSE

5 The Malaysian two-headed bat has a lump on its back that looks just like an extra head. This fools owls that attempt to bite the bat's head off in mid-air. TRUE/FALSE

6 The Indian climbing perch is a fish that climbs trees. TRUE/FALSE

WHAT ARE YOU DOING?

TREE FISHING

7 The Iberian 'singing' goat is an excellent mimic. (That's the posh name for someone who copies voices.) It has been known to imitate the yodelling calls of local mountaineers! TRUE/FALSE

8 There's a creature that hangs out in Australian rivers with a bill like a duck and fur like a beaver. It lays eggs like a bird and has poisonous spines like a lizard. TRUE/FALSE

ANSWERS

1 Probably false, although some people swear they've seen it. Maybe it's a relative of the more famous Loch Ness Monster. The Swedish government has banned attempts to kill or capture the creature just in case it does exist. **2** True. The horn is 15 cm long. The bird itself lives in marshes in tropical South America. You can hear its scream 3 km (2 miles) away. **3** True. **4** True. The golden tree snake can glide 46 metres. The snake launches itself from a high branch and draws its underside in and pushes its body forward as it zooms through the air. **5** False. **6** True. It uses its fins to grab branches. Once in the trees it allows ants to crawl over its body. Then it leaps back in the river. The ants fall off the fish and float around in the water – to be gobbled at leisure! **7** False. **8** True. It's the duck-billed platypus! This strange creature is actually an unusual species of mammal that looks like a mole pretending to be a duck. The puzzling platypus has also got detectors that sense electrical waves given off by small creatures at the bottom of muddy rivers. Classifying this freaky creature could drive a naturalist quackers.

NASTY NATURALISTS

Naturalists are scientists who study the natural world. Some study particular animals and others look at an entire habitat and its wildlife. Mind you, some naturalists have nasty habits. Here's a particularly eccentric example:

Hall of fame: Charles Waterton (1782–1865)
Nationality: British

Charles Waterton enjoyed pretending to be a mad dog and biting his visitors' ankles. A harmless youthful prank you might think, but cranky Chas was still playing this trick at the age of 57! Another curious habit was that he hated sleeping in a bed. He preferred a bare floor with a nice comfy block of wood for a pillow.

He made several trips to South America to find new types of animals – and then shot them. He stuffed their bodies so that he could study them at leisure. (He once captured an alligator alive by wrestling with it.) When at last he returned to his estate in England he spent £10,000 turning it into the world's first nature reserve. Yes, Waterton really liked animals – he even had his stables rebuilt so that the horses could 'talk' to one another.

Now you might think Waterton was barking mad – horses don't talk, do they? Animals are not nearly as clever as humans (including naturalists and teachers) or are they? Find out in the next chapter.

I ALWAYS FINISH IT OFF FOR THEM

DUMB ANIMALS?

So just how brainy are animals? And how good are their senses compared with our own? No one likes the idea that an animal might be brainier than themselves. That's why generations of nasty teachers have sunk to the depths of sarcasm.

YOU HAVE THE BRAIN OF A BIRD WILKINS, WHAT DO YOU SAY TO THAT?

TWEET, TWEET?

But what if your teacher said, "you have the brains of a horse,"? Well, you could reply that there was once a horse that answered maths questions.

The horse – Clever Hans – lived in Germany in the 1900s. When his owner asked a question, Hans would beat his hoof on the ground to spell out numbers. Sounds too brainy to be true? You're right – the owner leaned forward when Hans reached the right answer. The owner didn't mean to do this but clever Hans picked up the clue.

TEST YOUR TEACHER

So how does your teacher measure up against the best and brightest of the animal world? Can he or she decide how clever these animals really are?

1 In the 1970s, Ham Morris of Kentucky, USA tried to teach a horse named Butterscotch to drive a car. What do you think happened?
a) The horse couldn't get started.
b) The horse drove perfectly.
c) The horse crashed soon after getting a ticket for speeding.

2 Gorillas at Frankfurt Zoo, Germany, enjoy watching TV. What's their favourite viewing?
a) Soap operas.
b) Wildlife documentaries about other gorillas.
c) Sports programmes including the football results.

THE GIRAFFES SAY "CAN YOU RECORD IT FOR THEM, PLEASE?"

3 In 1913, a Mrs Moekel of Frankfurt, Germany, owned a dog who could solve maths questions by moving beads on an abacus — a type of counting frame. But how smart was the dog?
a) Stupid wasn't the word for him. He only knew his two times table up to 4 x 2 = 9 (or was it 8?).
b) The scientists found that the dog had been trained to do certain sums but had no mathematical understanding.
c) The dog could work out square roots and was smart enough to help Mrs Moekel's children with their maths homework.

4 Keepers at San Diego Zoo, California, USA, taught an Indian elephant to paint by holding a brush in her trunk. How good were these pictures?
a) They were masterpieces as good as some modern art. Copies now hang in the world's major art galleries.
b) They were terrible — just a load of pointless scribble. Mind you, some critics have hailed them as triumphs of 'post-modernist expressionism'.
c) They were recognizable pictures, but since the keepers were telling

the elephant what to do, they didn't count as the elephant's own work.

5 Scientists tested a chimp's intelligence by putting a blob of paint on its face and hanging a mirror in its room. The aim of the test was to see if the chimp realized the paint was on its face. What did the chimp do?
a) Looked in the mirror rather crossly and started rubbing the paint off its face.
b) Made faces at the mirror.
c) Tried to rub paint off the mirror.

6 British scientist Dr John Krebs added harmless amounts of a radioactive chemical to seeds and left them for marsh tits to hide and eat later. Then he used a Geiger

counter (a machine that detects radio-activity) to monitor the hidden seeds. What did he discover?

a) Birds are brainy. The marsh tits cleverly hid hundreds of seeds every day. And what's more, they were able to remember where they all were.

b) Bird-brained wasn't the word for them. The birds soon forgot where they had hidden the seeds.

c) Nothing. The experiment was called off after the scientist forgot where he'd left his Geiger counter.

7 A scientist decided to teach three octopuses to pull a light lever in their tank in return for a feed of fish. What happened?

a) The octopuses were too stupid to learn the simple trick.
b) The octopuses turned nasty and tried to strangle the scientist with their disgusting long tentacles.
c) They quickly learnt the trick but after a few days they became bored and went on strike.

ANSWERS

1b) The car had levers to control its movement and an accelerator pedal that the horse could step on. The horse operated the steering wheel with its muzzle. Mind you, the horse wasn't allowed out on the open road! 2 c) Obviously they thought that the games were the real monkey business! 3c) Amazing but true. The dog, a three-year-old Airedale terrier named Rolf, was tested by a group of scientists who found that his abilities were real. Could you do with a pet like this? 4c) Elephants also draw 'pictures' in the dust with their trunks but these really are meaningless scribbles. 5a) Chimps understand that the image they see in the mirror is their reflection. Monkeys do c) because they're not as smart as a chimp. How

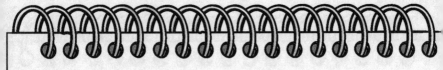

do you think your teacher would react first thing on a monday morning? 6a) But this is nothing. The North American nutcracker can hide up to 33,000 seeds — and find them again. 7c) They broke the light lever, squirted water at the scientist, and refused to take part in any more tests.

BET YOU NEVER KNEW!

Not all animals are clever. Some scientists reckon that the dumbest animal in the world is the turkey. Turkeys have been frightened to death by paper fluttering in the wind. Other turkeys have met nasty ends by cold or drowning because they're too stupid to shelter from the weather.

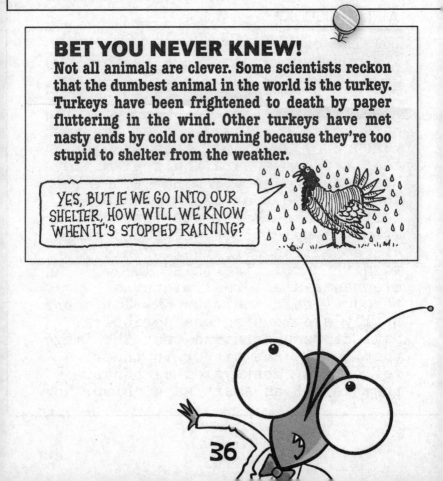

YES, BUT IF WE GO INTO OUR SHELTER, HOW WILL WE KNOW WHEN IT'S STOPPED RAINING?

FURRY FRIEND'S FEELINGS

For many years scientists believed animals didn't have feelings such as fear, anger and pride. But more recently they have begun to study this intriguing topic and they've come up with some freaky results. For example, baby elephants suffer from nightmares. Babies who have seen their parents killed by hunters wake up in the night crying. When they grow up these elephants sometimes attack humans as if seeking revenge. Is it because they 'never forget'?

As mentioned above, it's been said that elephants cry. There's a story that a circus elephant burst into tears after being hit by her cruel trainer. But boring old scientists point out that elephant's eyes water a lot anyway. Crocodiles weep too but for them it's a way of getting rid of unwanted salt. That's why we'll say someone's crying "crocodile tears" when they're just pretending to be sad.

NOW ARE YOU SURE THOSE AREN'T JUST CROCODILE TEARS?

Animals can feel happy. Gorillas supposedly sing when they're in a good mood. A singing gorilla sounds like a whining dog so it won't cheer up anyone else. Goats dance around and leap for joy when they're feeling chuffed. Perhaps instead of saying "happy bunny" we should say "happy goat" instead?

So it's official – animals are sensitive. But even if they didn't have feelings, they'd still be sensitive because animals have some pretty incredible senses, which they need to survive in their favourite habitats. But how do they measure up to humans? Surely they can't compete with us?

STUNNING SENSE STATISTICS

ANIMAL SENSES	HUMAN SENSES

SUPERSNIFFERS When you walk about in bare feet you leave 4 billionths of a gram of sweat in each footprint. To a dog this stinks like a cheesy old pair of socks that haven't been washed for a month.	**DON'T SMELL TOO WELL** A human's sense of smell is one million times weaker than a dog's. EVEN THOUGH HIS NOSE IS TWICE AS BIG 
EAGLE EYES A golden eagle can see a rabbit on the ground up to 3.2 km away.	**A SIGHT FOR SORE EYES** Some humans trip over rabbits.
A NASTY TASTE IN THE MOUTH Ugly catfish that lurk at the bottom of South American rivers have well over 250,000 taste buds in their tongues. That's how they find food in the murky mud.	**TOTALLY TASTELESS** Humans only have 10,000 taste buds – that's half as many as a pig. (This may explain why pigs don't enjoy school dinners but some humans do.)

HEAR, HERE

1. A dog's ear has at least 18 muscles so it can turn in any direction.

2. The Californian leaf-nosed bat can hear the footsteps of insects.

HARD OF HEARING HUMANS

1. Humans only have nine ear muscles and most people can't even waggle theirs.

2. Can you?

NO!

A TOUCH OF MAGIC

Seals use their ultra-sensitive whiskers to pick up tiny movements in the water caused by another creature.

A TOUCHY SUBJECT

Human whiskers don't even twitch.

IT'S TRUE!

STRANGE SENSES

1. Animals can predict earthquakes. In 2003, Japanese scientists found that mice behave oddly when they detect changes in magnetic forces linked to quakes.'

2. The American knife-fish produces an electric signal 300 times every second. This creates a force field around the animal. A disturbance in the field warns the fish there's another creature about.

SENSELESS

1. Weedy humans can't accurately predict earthquakes even using sophisticated scientific instruments.

2. Er ...

OK, YOU WIN!

DARE YOU DISCOVER ... HOW CATS SEE IN THE DARK?

You will need:
- 1 torch • 1 cat • 1 dark room

CAT

TORCH

What you do:

Allow the cat a few minutes to get used to the dark.

Shine the torch in the cat's eyes. What do you notice?

a) The cat doesn't notice the light.

b) The cat's eyes reflect back the light.

c) The cat's eyes glow red like a vampire's.

ANSWER

b) The cat has a layer of cells at the back of its eye that act like a mirror. These reflect light inside the eyeball and allow the cat to see better in the dark.

Hall of fame: Karl Von Frisch (1886–1982)
Nationality: Austrian

Karl was the son of a wealthy Austrian professor. He spent his childhood living in an old mill that his father was doing up and making friends with the local wildlife. He grew up to be a famous naturalist who discovered how bees pass on messages by doing little dances. Here's one of his nastiest investigations. Could you solve this problem as easily?

COULD YOU BE A NATURALIST?

Professor Otto Korner of Rostock University cut up fish and found that fish ears didn't work like human ears. So he reckoned fish were deaf. To prove his point he put some fish in a tank and whistled at them. The fish ignored him.

Finally, to prove his case Otto asked a famous singer to perform a private concert ... for the fish. She bawled out her operatic arias at an ear-splitting pitch. But still the fish took no notice!

Karl Von Frisch took an interest in this research and did his own tests. Imagine you were Karl Von Fish er, sorry, Frisch. What do you think you'd discover?

a) There's no doubt about it – fish are deaf as posts.

b) Don't be daft. It just proves that fish don't like boring old classical music.

c) Fish can hear but they're only interested in sounds to do with important things like food.

Are you sure they can't hear?

43

> ## ANSWER
>
> **c)** Karl blinded an unfortunate catfish and whistled every time he put some food on its nose. The fish tossed the food into its mouth. One day Karl whistled but didn't add the food. The fish reacted to the whistle by tossing its head. This is the reaction known to scientists as a conditioned reflex. The fish heard the whistle and learnt that it meant feeding time.

Many beasts aren't dumb animals at all. But what would they say to us if they could talk? Well, animals CAN talk ... in a manner of speaking.

WATCH ME TALK TO MY SICK DOG

HOW ARE YOU FEELING BONZO?

RUFF!

SNARLS, GROWLS AND HOWLS

Most animals communicate with one another to pass on nasty warnings or to show they're friendly. But creatures such as parrots can talk just like humans. Scientists say they're just copying the sound of the human voice. The animals don't realize what they're saying. Or do they?

CAN ANIMALS REALLY TALK?

Look at these examples and then decide for yourself.

A big-mouthed bird

For 12 years after 1965, the National Cage and Aviary Bird Show award for Best Talking Parrot-like bird was won by an African Grey parrot named Prudle. He knew over 800 words and even made up sentences. This amazed scientists who believed that parrots only copy what humans say.

WHEN ARE THEY GOING TO PUT SOME WATER IN THIS BIRD-BATH?

Who's a pretty boy then?

In 1980, Dr Irene Pepperburg of Purdu University, Indiana, USA, published a report on her research with an African Grey parrot named Alex. This brainy bird could ask for things such as a piece of paper to clean his beak. He knew the names of colours and shapes and even told Dr P that he felt miserable when he moulted (lost his feathers).

A sign of wisdom

In 1966, some American scientists tried to teach chimpanzees sign language for the deaf. One of the first apes to learn this was a female called Washoe. One day one of the researchers told Washoe that he'd just seen a big black dog with sharp teeth that ate baby chimps. Then he asked Washoe if she'd like to go outside. "NO!" signed Washoe nervously. After that whenever the scientists wanted Washoe to go indoors they told her that they'd seen the dog!

HA HA – IT WORKS EVERY TIME!

Despite falling for this nasty trick, Washoe proved to be a quick learner. She became so good at sign language she could even make up her own words such as 'drink-fruit' (melon) and 'water-bird' (swan).

SHE SAYS "YOUR HEAD LOOKS LIKE A MELON".

Washoe gave birth to a baby but sadly the infant fell sick and died at an animal hospital. The scientists came to tell Washoe what had happened.

"Where's baby?" signed the chimp.

"Baby finished," replied one of the researchers.

The poor mother retreated into a corner and wouldn't 'talk' to anyone for several days.

In 1979, Washoe adopted a baby chimp and began to teach him sign language. As they say, it's good to talk…

SPEAK FOR YOURSELF

Of course, when animals talk to one another they don't speak in human language. They've got their own forms of communication which can be quite complicated. Could you learn them?

TEACH YOURSELF LANGUAGE GUIDES

Liven up your holiday by talking to the wildlife. Now you can learn how to do this in the privacy of your own home. With these handy guides!

WHALE LANGUAGE
Have a 'whale' of a time as you learn to sing like a whale for up to 24 hours at a time. Learn to alter your song if you're addressing a female whale. Practise ultra-low noises that can be picked up by whales hundreds of kilometres away! Be careful, though, no one knows what these songs mean so let's hope the whales don't get too excited when you sing to them.

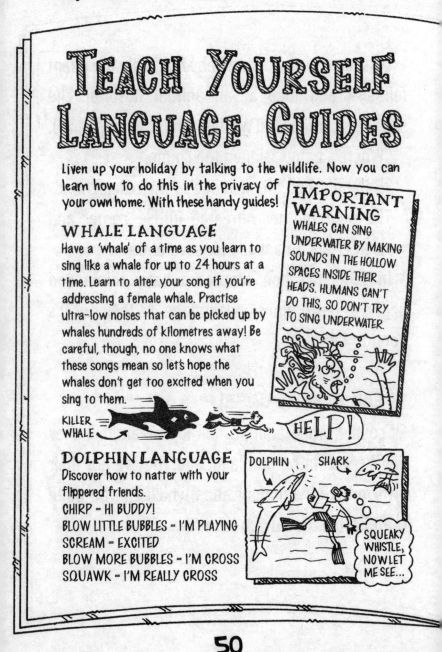

IMPORTANT WARNING
WHALES CAN SING UNDERWATER BY MAKING SOUNDS IN THE HOLLOW SPACES INSIDE THEIR HEADS. HUMANS CAN'T DO THIS, SO DON'T TRY TO SING UNDERWATER.

KILLER WHALE

HELP!

DOLPHIN LANGUAGE
Discover how to natter with your flippered friends.
CHIRP – HI BUDDY!
BLOW LITTLE BUBBLES – I'M PLAYING
SCREAM – EXCITED
BLOW MORE BUBBLES – I'M CROSS
SQUAWK – I'M REALLY CROSS

DOLPHIN   SHARK

SQUEAKY WHISTLE, NOW LET ME SEE...

GORILLA LANGUAGE

Ever wanted to gossip with a gorilla?
Here's a few words of gorilla language
to get you going!

WRAAGH! - DANGER!

GRUNT - BEHAVE YOURSELF (USED BY ADULT GORILLAS TOWARDS THEIR YOUNGSTERS.)

A BARKING HOOTING SOUND - I'M CURIOUS.

HOO, HOO, HOO - KEEP OUT!

BEATING CHEST - I'M BOSS.

HOO, HOO, HOO!

WRAAGH!

SPINY LOBSTER LANGUAGE

You'll need a comb and a finger for this one. Free comb with every
guide, but you'll have to use your own finger. Spiny lobsters rasp
their antennae against a sticking out part of their shells.

SLOW RASP - IT'S SAFE TO FEED.

RAPID RASP - TAKE COVER, THERE'S A SHARK ABOUT!

WHO'S THIS WEIRDO TELLING ME IT'S SAFE TO FEED?

MANUFACTURER'S WARNING

TO AVOID NASTY SCENES DON'T
PRACTISE YOUR ANIMAL SOUND
EFFECTS AT FAMILY MEAL TIMES.
FARMYARD IMPRESSIONS ARE
ALSO STRICTLY FORBIDDEN!

OINK, OINK!

I WISH HE WOULDN'T EAT LIKE A PIG

BET YOU NEVER KNEW!

Some of the loudest animal noises are made by South American howler monkeys. Their dawn cries warn other howler monkeys to keep off their rainforest territory. You can hear the howls 2 km away. Unfortunately, they can attract passing harpy eagles. The giant bird grabs an unsuspecting monkey in its claws and tears it to pieces.

COULD YOU BE A NATURALIST?

Vervet monkeys in Kenya have different alarm calls for leopards, eagles and snakes. A naturalist played these calls to the monkeys. What do you think they did?

a) Stuck their fingers in their ears and ignored the sounds.

b) The monkeys acted as if these dangerous animals were approaching.

c) The monkeys pelted the tape recorder with rotten fruit.

ANSWER

b) Leopard alarm – monkeys climbed the trees.
Eagle alarm – monkeys took cover under trees.
Snake alarm – monkeys checked the bushes.

COLOURFUL CHARACTERS

Some animals communicate without saying a word or making a sound. (Certain adults think that children should be able to do this too!)

1 The tilia fish of the Indian Ocean turns dark grey when it wants a scrap. If it loses, the fish turns white – maybe it's scared!

2 When the male tilia fish fancies a female his head turns brown, his jaw turns white and his fins become blood red.

3 Some humans turn an interesting shade of beetroot when they're cross, but did you know that octopuses are similar? A relaxed octopus is a tasteful shade of brown but an angry octopus turns red with rage.

4 Fiddler crabs turn red when they're cross, black when they're scared, and a rather fetching shade of purple when they meet a fiddler crab they fancy.

If you can't change colour, you can always tell people what you think by the look on your face. Birds, reptiles and fish can't make faces, but mammals can. We've all seen the nasty expression on a teacher's face. But did you know monkeys make faces, too? Famous naturalist, Charles Darwin, studied these fascinating faces.

Hall of fame: Charles Darwin (1809–1882)
Nationality: British
Charles Darwin nearly gave up science at an early age. At school scientific interests were not encouraged and young Charles once got told off for 'wasting time' on chemistry experiments. He later wrote:

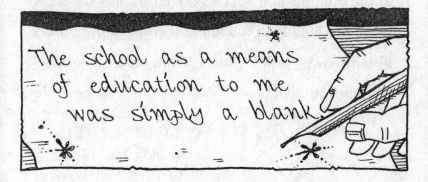

> The school as a means of education to me was simply a blank

Try quoting that to your science teacher!

But Charles followed his scientific interests and in 1858 announced his 'Theory of Evolution'. Studies of fossil bones showed that ancient animals looked different from today's creatures. So the new theory arrived to explain these changes. Darwin suggested:

1 That some animals survive and some get guzzled. (Amazing insight, that.) Naturalists call this grisly business "survival of the fittest". Well, you have to be pretty fit to escape from a hungry tiger.

2 The animals in a species are all slightly different from one another. (You look different to the others in your class, don't you? I mean, even a teacher can tell you apart.)

YES, SIMPKINS, IT IS TRUE THAT YOU LOOK SLIGHTLY DIFFERENT FROM OTHERS IN THE CLASS

3 Some animals in a species have features that give them a better chance of surviving. For example, take a bird like a nightjar. This bird is active at night and by day rests on the ground. Some nightjars are better camouflaged than the others. And you'll be glad to know they pass their crucial colouring on to their offspring.

4 After a while, you get more and more well-camouflaged nightjars because other nightjars are more easily spotted and scoffed by marauding cats.

5 This explains why after millions of years of evolution, each animal changes in appearance and ends up well-suited to its way of life. Either that, or dead.

At first, many people were appalled by Darwin's suggestion that humans had evolved from apes. But nowadays, Darwin's theory is accepted by many scientists as they continue to figure out how evolution operates.

FOR EXAMPLE, THE DODO
DID NOT SURVIVE BECAUSE:
1. IT COULDN'T FLY
2. IT WAS EASY TO CATCH
3. PEOPLE ATE IT

DARE YOU DISCOVER ... HOW TO TALK TO AN APE?

Here are some gestures you might find useful when you meet a monkey. You could practise them in front of a mirror (but not during a science lesson).

1 Kissing gesture:
Meaning: Help me please, I'm a friend.
Note: If a monkey makes this gesture it's a good idea to copy it. Hopefully you won't actually have to kiss the monkey.

2 Smacking lips:
Meaning: I love you and I want to eat the bits of dead skin and ticks in your hair.
Note: Monkeys do this to their friends. So if you smack lips to a monkey you better be serious about it.

3 Teeth chattering:
Meaning: HELP! I'm scared!
Note: Does anyone else have this effect on you?

DARE YOU DISCOVER ... HOW TO TALK TO YOUR PET DOG/CAT?

If you don't happen to have a pet monkey, you may look out for these expressions on a pet dog or cat.

1 EXCITED EYES Blinking eyes = I'm upset

2 FEARFUL FROWN

Frown. (Eyebrows lowered and eyes half-closed) = There's danger ahead

3 A CROSS CREATURE

Eyebrows down but eyes wide open = I don't like you. Note: It's always extremely rude to stare at a cat or dog. They get upset and if they happen to be much larger than you they might decide to take a chunk out of you.

4 EAGER EARS

Sideways ears = I'm resting

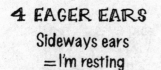

Twitching ears = I'm about to pounce.

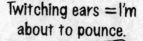

Floppy ears = I surrender!

5 MYSTERIOUS MOUTH

Mouth open but you can't see teeth = Let's play

Mouth tightly closed = I'm relaxed

Front teeth exposed =
I'm the boss.

All the teeth exposed =
You're the boss but I don't
like you and I'm going to
get you one day when I'm
feeling really brave.

IMPORTANT NOTE – You'd
better 'talk' nicely to your
pet otherwise it might go
wandering. You see,
some animals have a
nasty urge to drop
everything and go on their
travels.

TERRIBLE TRAVELS

Just like humans, some animals enjoy travelling, and others prefer to stay put. But animals don't travel for fun or holidays. Oh, no. They're searching for food, shelter or a mate. And some of their travels are definitely on the nasty side. Luckily, some animals aren't too fussy about where they stay.

A NASTY WAY TO GO

Just think of the nastiest, the hottest, the coldest or the WORST journey you've ever made. Now imagine making the same trip but with everything and everyone giant-sized, except you. And somewhere close by, large hungry creatures are waiting to pounce… Scared? That's how it feels to be a small animal on the move.

Yet amazingly, some animals make huge journeys – and can even find their way home from great distances with amazing accuracy. Impossible? How's this for a tall tail – er, tale?

Until 1952 headmaster Stacey Wood lived in California, USA. In that year he retired to a farm in Oklahoma – 3,000 km away. The whole family went except for the cat, Sugar, who was sent to live with neighbours. One year later a cat turned up at the Woods' new home. It was thin and bedraggled as if it had been on a long and desperate journey.

MIAOW!

INCREDIBLE!! I THINK IT'S SUGAR

WELL HE CAN WAIT UNTIL MORNING – I'VE JUST GOT INTO BED

Amazingly, against all the odds, the new arrival was Sugar, who had disappeared a few weeks after the family had left California. The cat even had Sugar's bad hip. For an entire year the courageous cat had trekked across the United States to find its family. And to this day no one knows how Sugar did it.

Other animals are also brilliant at finding their way. Take pigeons, for example.

PIGEON POWER

Now you might think a pigeon is a silly-looking bird with a tiny little head and a puny little brain to match. And of course, you'd be right. But when it comes to travelling, pigeons and many other birds are geographical geniuses.

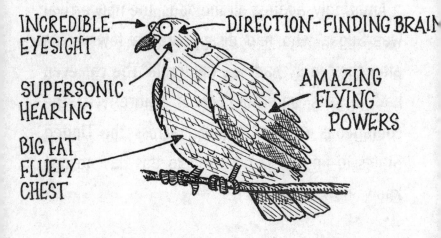

INCREDIBLE EYESIGHT

DIRECTION-FINDING BRAIN

SUPERSONIC HEARING

AMAZING FLYING POWERS

BIG FAT FLUFFY CHEST

1 Pigeons can fly all day at speeds of 48 km per hour (30 mph) and cover 1,120 km and still not get tired.

2 Pigeons' brains contain magnetic crystals sensitive to the Earth's magnetic field. This allows a pigeon to know which direction is north and which direction is home. This was proved in the 1970s when a scientist tied a magnet to a pigeon's head. The magnet confused the pigeon's crystals and the poor pigeon got lost.

3 Like other birds that fly long distances, pigeons can recognize landmarks and use the position of the sun and the stars to work out directions. They can even see rays of sunlight when the sun is behind a cloud.

4 And if that's not enough, pigeons hear sounds too low for us to hear. These strange sounds include earth movements and distant waves. Scientists think that pigeons can recognise places by the ultra-low sounds they hear.

5 With all these amazing abilities you won't be surprised to hear that a homing pigeon that wins races is worth its weight in gold. One such bird, Emerald, was sold in 1988 for £77,000 and even her eggs were worth £2,400 each. Drop a few of those and you could make the world's most expensive omelette.

But pigeons are just one species of high-flying, long-distance-travelling birds. Lots of birds migrate or travel from one area to another – every year. They do this because they have a powerful urge to fly off in a certain direction to find more food or a suitable nesting site. But scientists don't really understand how and why the birds manage it. Would you enjoy a holiday like this?

WING~IT HOLIDAYS

SWIFT TOURS

Air tours of sunny south-east Africa. Get away from the nasty British winter. Non-stop air flights with in-flight refreshments. Just catch yourself a few crunchy insects on the way. Exclusive washing facilities – just whiz through a thunderstorm. Note to passengers: the trip covers 19,200 km and we won't be landing at all. Not even to visit the toilet.

WANDERING ALBATROSS TOURS

Antarctica is the last unspoilt continent on Earth. Now you can fly around its beautiful coast in search of fish. Enjoy panoramic views and a lovely smooth ride. Your wandering albatross pilot can glide for six days without beating a wing. In-flight meals include mouth-watering raw fish – with that 'just caught' taste.

ARCTIC TERN TOURS

A holiday with a difference. Good weather is guaranteed! Yes, you can be sure that every day will 'tern' out nice again! Escape the northern winter blues by flying direct to sunny Antarctica where the days are warmest at this time of year. Then back to the Arctic in time for summer. Lovely fish suppers are available all the way, too.

THE NASTIEST ANIMAL JOURNEYS

Other animals, besides birds, also migrate. Their journeys are full of difficulties and dangers. Here's some of the nastiest examples. Would you want to tag along with this lot?

Ambling amphibia

Every year thousands of fearless frogs and not-so-timid toads return to the ponds where they hatched as tadpoles. They do this to mate and lay eggs. Unfortunately, they often try to hop across roads without looking and end up squashed by cars. Sometimes they get there only to find humans have drained their pond. In other places, however, naturalists have built tunnels under the roads so the wandering wildlife can cross safely.

Sociable snakes

Every year, 20,000 red garter snakes slither 16 km from their summer homes in the marshes of Manitoba, Canada, to their winter hideaways in sheltered rocky pits. After the winter they return to the marshes. Nothing too nasty about that – as long as you don't mind the sight of thousands of snakes. The snakes insist on taking short cuts through people's homes and often inspect their dinner tables.

Loony lemmings

Lemmings are small furry animals that happily scamper about in the Arctic snow. But every 3–4 years things get difficult. A rapid rise in lemming numbers means there isn't enough food to go round. So the lemmings form a huge army and attack anything in their way – including humans. They even do crazy things like trying to swim wide rivers. Where are they going? The lemmings don't know. There's an old story that lemmings leap off cliffs during these migrations – but it's not true. That would be too crazy – even for a lemming!

Terrible turtle treks

Every year, green turtles swim to Ascension Island in the Atlantic Ocean to lay their eggs. No one knows why they go there but the island has few large animals that want to eat the turtles. Unfortunately, the island is only 13 km by 9 km in size and some turtles have to swim 2,080 km to get there. To make matters worse the tired turtles' top speed is only 3 km (less than 2 miles) an hour.

A slippery trip

For 15 years a European eel does nothing very much except squirm around in a muddy river or pond. Every so often it scrunches a passing fish and that's it for excitement. Then one day the eel starts feeling eel – er sorry, ill. It turns from yellow to silver and its eyes bulge.

Its snout gets longer and – eel-longated (ha ha). Then the eel develops an irresistible urge to swim to the sea. So strong is this feeling that an eel will even slither to the nearest river over dry land. The eel swims the length of the river to the sea and wriggles up to 4,000 km to the Sargasso Sea – a vast area of seaweed in the Atlantic Ocean.

When it gets there … the exhausted eel dies. Bit of a wasted effort you might think – except that just before it dies the eel mates. Its offspring (called elvers), tiny see-through eels, set off for home. Without any help they find their way to the rivers and ponds of Europe.

And guess what? No one knows how eels came to develop this amazing lifestyle or how they find their way on their mysterious migrations.

No matter how far it has to go, every animal's body is suited to getting around. That's why dolphins have flippers, birds have wings and frogs are champion hoppers. Here's your chance to get moving on this topic.

DARE YOU DISCOVER ... HOW YOU MEASURE UP TO A GIBBON?

How good are you at brachiation (brake-ee-ay-shun)? If your answer is, "my bike brakes are fine," you ought to know that brachiation means leaping from branch-to-branch. It's a dangerous way of getting to school in the morning. But gibbons brachiate all the time. That's not surprising, really – gibbons are apes that live in the trees of south-east Asia.

Here's the secret of their success:

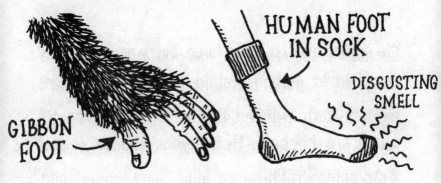

GIBBON FOOT

HUMAN FOOT IN SOCK

DISGUSTING SMELL

Take a look at this gibbon's foot. Now compare it to your own right foot. (It helps if you take off your sock.) What do you notice?

a) Nothing. My foot is exactly the same.

b) The gibbon's big toe looks more like my thumb.

c) The gibbon's toes are shorter.

ANSWER

b) Unlike your feet, a gibbon's feet aren't good at walking on the ground. But they're very good at gripping small branches. Can you do this with your big toe? Gibbons have long arms and strong shoulder muscles to hurl themselves from branch to branch.

Eventually, though – just like you at the end of a hard day in the classroom – every animal's thoughts turn to home. But for an animal, 'home' isn't a place to watch TV or play computer games. It's somewhere to store food, raise young and shelter from larger, fiercer creatures. Bet you wouldn't feel at home in any of these places.

NASTY HOME TRUTHS

1 The Australian white tree frog is a friendly little creature with a big smile on its slimy face. Clearly, this happy hopper is very pleased with its favourite home – a toilet cistern. (Before the invention of the toilet the frogs lived in smelly ponds.)

2 Snapping turtles in eastern North America are quite at home in smelly stagnant ponds or stinking sewers. It's a bad idea to go paddling in these places (as if you would!). Snapping turtles lurk in the shallows and they'd love nice pink toes for tea.

DON'T WORRY – NOTHING WOULD LIVE IN A SMELLY STAGNANT PLACE LIKE THIS...

3 An octopus will live in any hollow object lying on the sea bed. They're really not fussy – for a small octopus a human skull makes a cosy little home.

4 Eagles and ospreys build large, scruffy twig nests on top of trees. Unfortunately, they also build them on electricity pylons. Sometimes a bird touches a power line and you end up with Kentucky fried eagle.

5 Cave swiftlets are birds related to swifts that live, not surprisingly, in caves. Their nests are made from bits of plants glued together with … spit. Yes – swiftlet spit sets swift-ly (ha, ha!) to form a strong glue. And this is added to chicken and spices to make traditional Chinese bird's nest soup. Oddly enough, swiftlets eat something similar. They feed their young on balls of insects glued together with tasty all-purpose spit. Yummmeee!

Of course, not all animals build their own homes. It's too much like hard work. Some move into other animals' homes instead. For example, North American black-tailed prairie dogs are squirrel-like creatures that dig a maze of tunnels to live in. Some of these tunnel systems are huge, with up to 50 entrances. Soon unwelcome lodgers move in –

these include owls, squirrels, salamanders, mice, black-footed ferrets and even the odd rattlesnake. And that's not the only way that animals take advantage of one another. Some do nasty things like – eating their hosts alive, or slurping their blood. Yikes! Read on if you dare…

THE NEXT CHAPTER'S REALLY GRUESOME!

NICE AND NASTY: HELPERS AND HANGERS ON

When different animals get together, things happen. Nice things and nasty things. Some animals help one another and some animals are just harmless hangers on ... but others try to help themselves at the expense of other creatures.

ANIMAL AIDERS

The idea of animals doing one another good turns sounds odd – doesn't it? But it shouldn't. After all, we keep pet dogs and cats – or even pet toads and snakes. Pets keep us company, often show us affection and leave little puddles on the carpet. In return, we feed them and provide shelter. And other animals such as horses and sheepdogs work for us in return for more food and shelter. When animals help one another this is known as symbiosis (sim-by-o-sis).

BET YOU NEVER KNEW!

Animals raised by humans sometimes keep pets. One of the apes taught to 'speak' using sign language in America, was Koko the gorilla. Now Koko was happy living with researcher Dr Francine 'Penny' Patterson. But the gorilla had one wish. More than anything else – she wanted a kitten of her own. So in 1984, kind-hearted Dr Patterson gave her one.

Koko called her new pet 'All Ball'. She treated All Ball as her baby and even dressed it in cute little hats and scraps of material. Koko often tried to get the kitten to tickle her. (The gorilla enjoyed being tickled by her human friends.) And when the kitten was well-behaved Koko signed that it was a 'soft good cat'. Altogether now – Ahhhh. But if you like happy endings don't read the bit below.

Soon after, All Ball was run over and killed. Boo hoo! Poor Koko was heart-broken and nothing could cheer her up until Dr Patterson bought her another kitten.

FEATHERED FRIENDS

1 There's one little bird in Africa that's fond of beeswax and the juicy grubs that wriggle around in the sticky honeycomb. But how to get it – that's the problem. The honey is protected by thousands of bad-tempered bees.

So the bird calls to attract a passing honey badger. Then the bird flies towards the bees' nest.

The badger has learnt to follow the bird's signals. The bees can't sting the badger's thick skin as it claws open the nest. Meanwhile, the bird gobbles up any spare honeycomb.

YUMMY HONEY!

And the name of this bird? The honeyguide bird.

2 Another African bird, the oxpecker, rides on the backs of hippo, zebras and rhinos. The larger animals don't mind. The bird eats the flies that infest their backs. And it even warns of approaching humans. If the larger animal takes no notice, the bird drums its beak against their head.

HOME HELPERS

Some creatures help each other by providing homes in return for services rendered.

For most fish, getting mixed up in the poisonous tentacles of a Portuguese man-o-war (a jellyfish-like creature) is something they wouldn't live to regret – because they wouldn't live much longer.

But for one fish this is home. Nomeus (no-me-us) is a little fish that lives amongst the tentacles, protected from harm by its extra slimy skin. The fish keeps the tentacles nice and clean. When other fish try to catch Nomeus they fall victim to the jellyfish – and Nomeus gets to eat the leftovers.

In a cosy, sandy burrow at the bottom of the sea live a pair of oddly-matched housemates – Luther's goby fish and the blind shrimp. The shrimp digs his burrow and the goby guides his friend on feeding trips. The shrimp keeps his antenna on the fish's tail. If there's danger, goby wags his tail and the two friends run off home.

But helping each other and looking after one another isn't all that animals do. Some even clean one another. And there's a great choice of cleaners – if you don't mind being nibbled.

CREATURE COMFORTS SERVICES DIRECTORY

HEY FISH – D'YOU FANCY A WASH AND BRUSH UP?

Let your friendly cleaner wrasse do the job for you. We'll nibble that nasty mould and fungus away and leave your scales as good as new! Speedy personal attention assured.

ALMOST FINISHED

"Cleaner wrasse managed to serve a queue of 300 fish in a single session. Highly recommended."

A. Shark (Pacific Ocean)

WARNING!
To all customers of Cleaner wrasse Services: BEWARE OF CHEAP IMITATIONS! Blenny fish try to copy Cleaner wrasse. They've even copied the stripe on our bodies. But BEWARE! As soon as they get close they'll take a bite out of you and scarper!

GOBIES' GROUPER GOB-GROOMING SERVICES

Are you a grouper fish with bad breath? Special offer – let us clean out your mouth free of charge! We'll eat those nasty bits of rotten food and we won't leave you feeling down in the mouth.

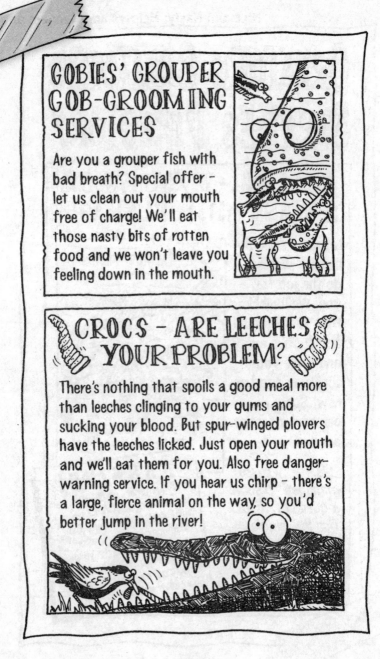

CROCS – ARE LEECHES YOUR PROBLEM?

There's nothing that spoils a good meal more than leeches clinging to your gums and sucking your blood. But spur-winged plovers have the leeches licked. Just open your mouth and we'll eat them for you. Also free danger-warning service. If you hear us chirp – there's a large, fierce animal on the way, so you'd better jump in the river!

COULD YOU BE A NATURALIST?

In coral reefs, fish cleaning is done by shrimps from special areas known as 'cleaning stations'. A scientist removed all the shrimps from a cleaning station. Can you guess what happened next?

a) The fish started nibbling one another in a vain attempt to keep clean.

b) Nothing. The fish weren't bothered whether they were dirty or not.

c) The fish went away in search of another cleaning station.

ANSWER

c) The fish staged a mass walk-out. Or should that be a swim-out?

WHERE ARE THEY?

DON'T ASK ME, I'M A PRAWN

PESKY PARASITES

But not all creatures are helpful. Some couldn't be helpful in a month of Sundays. They're known as parasites – animals that don't hunt for food, but steal it in various horrible ways from other creatures. These parasites do their victims no favours at all. Which of these parasites would you least want to meet?

Frigate birds of Central America have an unusual method of getting a free lunch. They wait until another bird has caught a fish then chase their victim and force them to sick up their meal. The foul frigate bird then gulps the sick in mid-air. And if that isn't nasty enough, they also steal eggs and eat other birds' chicks – including baby frigate birds.

European cuckoos lay their eggs in other birds' nests. The cuckoo hatches and chucks the other fledglings out of the nest. The parents feed the cuckoo and don't even notice any difference. Not even when the cuckoo grows up to five times their size. (Would your parents notice if you were replaced by another creature?) As soon as it's fully grown the cuckoo takes off for a lovely winter holiday in Africa. And guess what? It doesn't even say "thank you!".

I MEAN, DO I REALLY LOOK LIKE A SPARROW?

Sea lampreys have been described as 'a yard of garden hosepipe that's been left out all winter'. And that's putting it nicely. These foul fish have no mouth or teeth – just suckers and fangs, and they like nothing better than sucking the blood of other fish.

Want to know something really scary? There's something that lurks in the South American jungle that makes other parasites seem almost OK. Oh yes, this is much, much worse. D'you want to know what it is? Turn down the lights, close the shutters and draw close to the fire.

WHAT'S EATING YOU?

"But when did it happen, grandpa?" asked the young boy with his eyes like saucers.

"It was in Brazil, back in 1927. We were there to study the wildlife and it was my first time in the jungle. I remember the nights – the humming insects and the croaking frogs in the dank, smelly swamps. We made camp around nightfall. Old Dr Beebe's orders. That's William Beebe of the New York Zoological Society – our expedition leader. And Dr B said we should always keep our feet inside the tents."

"Why did he say that, Grandpa?"

"Well, because of the vampires, of course," hissed the old man.

"Vampires? Not real vampires like Count Dracula?" The boy's voice rose higher.

"Dracula wasn't no real vampire, Johnnie. He was a legend. But this is true. As true as I'm sitting here. Real live vampire bats."

The young boy gulped.

"Bats! And do they really bite people?" he stammered.

"Sure they do — and animals like cows and horses. Not dogs so much. Dogs can hear 'em coming. The bats flap down from the trees where they live — silent as ghosts. They've got wings like old leather and huge ears to hear with. They creep along the ground to find your feet. Then they lick your toes to make sure they're nice and soft. And then they bite you!"

The boy looked over his shoulder nervously. "Do they really suck blood?"

"No, they lap it up like a cat laps milk. Or at least that's what Dr Beebe told us. He was always going on about bats."

"Well, it was soon after that I got a rude awakening. I was in a deep long sleep. Suddenly, I felt a sharp pain in my big toe like a needle. I shouted and then I was awake. Sweat streamed off me like a waterfall. It was dark but there was a moon and I saw ... a creature crouching over me...

"Well, I was terrified. Somehow I switched on my torch and what do you think I saw? It was Dr Beebe. He was holding a bright, sharp pin.

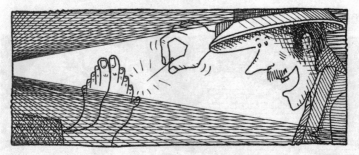

"'Sorry about that,' he chuckles. 'Just trying a little test – I wanted to know if a vampire bat would wake you up.'"

"Looks like it would." I said crossly.

"It turned out Dr B played the same trick on everyone. 'Practical research' he called it although the guys called it something else. Well, the following night I slept really well. Must have been the rude interruption the night before. When I woke up I felt fine. Until I looked at my feet and saw the blood. Those pesky vampire bats had come by – and I hadn't felt a thing!"

BET YOU NEVER KNEW!

1 There are three species of vampire bats. They are currently a big problem in Brazil because they can pass on deadly diseases such as rabies to the animals they bite. But they do have one good habit. The bats are spotlessly clean. They always lick the dried blood off their fur before selecting their next victim.

2 A vampire bat needs to drink its weight in blood every night in order to survive. That's like you having to slurp a bath of steaming hot blood for your supper.

Mind you – there's one thing worse than being picked on by a blood-sucking bat. And that's having lunch with a horribly hungry hunter. Especially when it's YOU on the menu!

HORRIBLE HUNTERS

When you're hungry you probably pop out to the shops to buy food. It's called "shopping". Animals can't usually do this so, instead, they pop out and nab some unfortunate, small creature for their tea. Here's how they do it.

HORRIBLE HUNTER TYPES

Some hunters, such as lions and tigers, eat large animals. For them life is rather relaxing. They spend most of their life sleeping off huge meals. They only hunt when they're really hungry. It helps to keep out of their way at these times. Other hunters, such as wild dogs or hyenas, will eat anything that comes along and they're always on the look out for a free lunch. Best avoid them at all times.

And beware. Hunters play horrible tricks.

HORRIBLE HUNTER TRICKS

1 Sneak up on your victim. If they turn round freeze and pretend to be a twig. The olive green snake of Central America does this. It even sways in the breeze – before it strikes and grabs a poor little baby bird from its nest.

THEY HAVEN'T TWIGGED YET

2 The horned frog sits motionless except for one finger. This twitches until an insect or small creature comes by thinking it's something to eat. Big mistake. It's feeding time all right – feeding time for the frog.

3 There's a type of African mongoose with a bottom that looks like a small flower. The mongoose crouches on a shrub with its bum in the air. When an insect lands on the pretty 'flower' the mongoose whips round and snaps it up.

4 White-coated polar bears are almost invisible against the Arctic snow. But the bear's large black nose is embarrassingly obvious when it sneaks up on a seal. So the bears push a lump of ice in front of them to hide their tell-tale noses.

5 Everyone knows that rattlesnakes have a rattle at the end of their tails. Some of their few fans say that the rattle is there to warn people to steer clear. Huh – as if snakes are that thoughtful. In fact, the rattle is there to attract attention away from the head with its fatal fangs.

Could you be as cunning as these horrible hunters? Now's your chance to find out. Imagine you were a lioness living on the plains of Southern Africa. What sort of a hunter would you make?

LION HUNTING TIPS

The lionesses in a pride (group of lions) hunt together. (The lazy males don't take part.)

1 Your pride of lionesses stalk a herd of gazelles (small antelope). From what direction do you approach?
a) With the wind at your back so that the gazelles can smell you. This will scare them so much they won't be able to defend themselves.
b) With the wind blowing in your face so the gazelles can't smell you.
c) From the direction of the sun so that the gazelles are dazzled.

2 Your pride splits into two groups. What do you do next?
a) One group charges the gazelles

and chases them towards the second group waiting in ambush.

b) One group goes after the gazelles and the others chase some nearby zebra. This doubles the chance of catching something.

c) One group chases gazelles and the others keep watch for marauding hyenas that might try to steal the meat.

3 You select a gazelle to attack. Which one do you choose?

a) The biggest — more meat for you.

b) The smallest — less likely to put up a fight.

c) The weakest — easier to catch.

4 The males invite themselves to the feast. While you and your sisters have been hunting the males have been lazing about in the sun. Now they're hungry. So who gets the lion's share?

a) The lionesses, followed by the cubs. The males are given a few scraps. Serves 'em right for not helping.

b) The males take the best bits. The

lionesses and the cubs get what's
left. If they're lucky.
c) The cubs. After all they need the
food to help them grow.

5 A new male chases away the old
males in your pride. He cruelly kills
and eats your cubs. What do you do?
a) Run for the hills.
b) Kill him and eat his body.
c) Make friends with him.

6 In the dry season there's little
food. What do you eat?
a) Other lions
b) Fish, insects, lizards, mice and
the odd tortoise.
c) Bones buried for just such an
emergency.

ANSWERS

Give yourself one point for each correct answer. **1 b)**. **2 a)** Lions show a lot of teamwork when hunting. Some scientists believe that this is an illusion and all the lions are doing their own thing. **3 c)**. **4 b)** Males are bigger and stronger than the females. If there's not enough food for everyone the lionesses and cubs starve. **5 c)** Nasty but true. The male wants the lioness to look after his youngsters once they are born. The lioness wants the male to protect her from other males. **6 b)** A starving lion will eat anything, so be careful if you're in the area.

WHAT YOUR SCORE MEANS:

5–6 A roar of approval. You'd make a great hunter.

3–4 You're mane-ly right but you need to lick your skills into shape.

1–2 You'll never be a lion. Best swallow your 'pride' and stick to being a human.

COULD YOU BE A NATURALIST?

One fierce hunter from the African plains is the cheetah. These big cats are the fastest creatures on Earth and reach speeds of 105 km an hour (65 mph) in short bursts. The problem is that a racing cheetah's muscles produce huge amounts of heat. If the cheetah ran at top speed for more than a few seconds it would suffer fatal brain damage. A puffed-out cheetah needs to put its paws up for a few minutes to recover.

In 1937, an animal collector staged races between a cheetah and a greyhound in London. What do you think happened?

a) The greyhound won.

b) The cheetah ate the greyhound.

c) The cheetah won but only sometimes. Most of

the time she couldn't be bothered to make the effort.

ANSWER

c) Cheetahs don't participate well in races. In another race in 1937 a cheetah only completed half the course and then took a breather.

FAR-FETCHED FISH FACTS

So far all the hunters we've been talking about have been land hunters. But that doesn't mean you'd be safe underwater — especially if you're edible. The seas and rivers swarm with millions of ferocious fish. Which of these fish is too nasty to be true?

1 A trumpet fish hitches a ride on a larger but harmless parrot fish. When the trumpet fish spots a small fish to eat it hops off to make a quick killing! True/false

2 Vicious blue fish attack schools of other fish off the Eastern coasts of North America. The brutal blues kill more than ten times the fish they can eat. They guzzle up to 40 at a time and then sick them up so they can go on eating! True/false

3 The halitosis haddock has a deadly and unusual weapon — its disgusting, smelly breath. When a smaller fish comes by, the horrible haddock

breathes a cloud of poisonous bubbles to overwhelm its prey. True/false

4 The angler fish has its own fishing rod complete with a small worm-like object that dangles just above its mouth. When another fish comes to investigate the bait the angler fish snaps up its catch. True/false

5 The scissors fish has jaws just like a pair of scissors and it uses these fearsome weapons to slice up its prey. It's even been known to snip through the lines of deep sea anglers. True/false

6 The deep sea viper fish has 1,350 lights inside its mouth. They twinkle in the ocean depths and little fish flock to see the lovely spectacle. Once the fish are inside its mouth the viper fish closes its giant gob. End of show. True/false

ANSWERS
3, 5 False, 1, 2, 4, 6 True.

BET YOU NEVER KNEW!

One fierce fish that's all too real is the great white shark. Did you know it senses movements in the water up to 1.6 km away? At 400 metres the shark can also sniff blood. It usually sneaks up behind or below its victim. At the last moment, the shark closes its cold black eyes and homes in on its victim's terrified heartbeat. Yes – the heartbeat produces tiny electrical waves and the shark senses these. Then it's GRAB-A-BITE time!

COULD YOU BE A NATURALIST?

The archer fish of India, Australia and Southeast Asia has an unusual secret weapon. A built-in water pistol. This 2-cm-long fish spits water with deadly accuracy at passing insects.

SORRY! I WAS AIMING FOR THE FLY

A public aquarium once kept a school of the fish and splatted 150 g of raw meat on the sides of their tank. The owner wanted to see if the fish could dislodge the food. Could they?

a) These fish are little squirts. So they couldn't budge the meat.

b) The fish kept squirting until all the meat was in the water.

c) Unable to shift the meat by squirting the fish leapt up and grabbed it in their tiny jaws.

ANSWER

b) Yes – they certainly made a big splash.

One of the fiercest hunters is one that you may have met already. Indeed this ferocious creature may be lurking behind your curtains or even watching your TV! Yes – we're talking about your not-so-cuddly cat. Here's where we let the cat out of the bag. Your pet leads a deadly double-life.

TIDDLES THE TERRIBLE

Tiddles rubs your legs. Just trying to be friendly? No way. She's leaving her scent on you to show you're part of HER family.

THAT'S MY GIRL

Tiddles has her own hunting territory. Normally she won't allow any other cat into this area. The territory is a little larger than your garden.

BOUNDARY LINE →

GET LOST!

Tiddles hunts by sneaking up on prey. Sometimes she freezes before moving stealthily forward once more. At the last moment she pounces.

FREEZE POSITION   POUNCE POSTURE

Tiddles enjoys catching insects. They have such a lovely crunchy texture – it's just like you eating crisps.

BIZZ BUZZ

But she doesn't like catching rabbits or rats. She's scared of rabbits because they're so big. And she thinks that rats taste worse than cheap cat food.

When Tiddles 'plays' with mice she's not being cruel. Oh no? She's just a big scaredy-cat. Scared the mouse will fight back (some mice do). So she keeps her distance without losing the mouse.

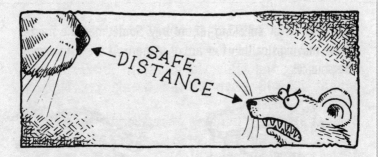

Tiddles eats mice head first. Gulp. Before eating birds she plucks out the feathers with her teeth.

1ST COURSE = MOUSE

2ND COURSE
(ALREADY
PREPARED) = BIRD

When Tiddles brings you a half-dead mouse or battered bird it's her way of teaching you to hunt. Yes — she wants you to finish it off. Mother cats do this to train their kittens.

ARRRGH!

MUST BE SOME SORT OF BATTLE CRY BEFORE HE JUMPS ON IT

BET YOU NEVER KNEW!

1 The champion hunter of all time was a cat named Towser. By the time she died in 1987 she had caught 28,899 mice at the Glenturret Whisky Distillery, Scotland.

2 A cat's skill in hunting once saved a man's life. The man in question was Sir Henry Wyatt, a 15th-century English knight who was locked in a dungeon and left to starve. But hungry Henry was befriended by a stray cat. The cat brought in birds such as pigeons and kept the knight alive until he was released by friends.

Mind you, if cats have ambitions, it must be every cat's dream to be a really big cat. A really big cat and a really deadly hunter. Something like a tiger, in fact.

TERRIBLE TIGERS

From its nose to the tip of its stripy tail the average tiger is 2.9 metres long and weighs 204 kg – that's the weight of three grown men. In the 19th century, Victorian writers gave the tiger a bad press. They saw the tiger as a treacherous enemy that took its victims by surprise. The Hon James Inglis wrote:

... the tiger is ... a cunning, sneaking rogue ... a cruel, whiskered robber.

Nineteenth-century hunters enjoyed 'bagging' tigers and they even got paid for their horrible pastime by the Indian government! Many tigers ended up as grisly tiger-skin rugs. But the hunters were far too deadly for the tigers. By 1972 there were only about 1,800 tigers left alive in the whole of India. Hunting was banned in 1971 and thanks to a massive conservation effort, tiger numbers began to increase in some areas. But the naturalists' work raised a nasty dilemma. Some tigers can kill humans. These days, when this happens the tiger isn't killed, it's moved away from where people live…

TIGER TRACKER'S TIPS

Here are some tips to avoid being eaten by a man-eating tiger. (Hopefully there aren't too many around where you live.)

1 A tiger tries to creep up on you from downwind. Always keep an eye out for movements from that direction.

2 A tiger is more likely to attack you if you crouch down. It thinks you're a four-legged animal rather than a human. So it's a very bad idea to squat down to go to the toilet in the jungle.

3 Tigers attack from behind you. In 1987 people living in the forests on the borders of India and Bangladesh were issued with plastic face masks to wear over the backs of their heads. Tiger attacks virtually stopped because the tigers thought people were looking at them when their backs were turned. It was the next best thing to eyes in the back of their heads.

WHY HAS EVERYONE STARTED RUNNING BACKWARDS?

4 If a tiger's after you and you've left your mask at home, the best thing to do is to climb a tree. Most tigers can't climb trees.

5 Tigers always attack the neck. For a person bitten by a tiger it's all over. The chances of getting away are one in a hundred. Yikes! Now you might think that tigers or the humans that shoot them are the nastiest hunters. But you'd be wrong. Think of beady little eyes.

POISONED PREY

Snakes. Ugh! *They're* nasty enough, but there's a whole army of other horrible hunters that also use poison. Why do they do it? Is it to scare us? Well – no, but it's a very effective way of bumping off smaller creatures. As you're about to find out.

Nasty nature fact file

Name: Snakes
The basic facts: Snakes are reptiles without legs. They
                            come in 2,500 varieties – but only 600
                            are poisonous. The good news is that
                            only 150 types of snake can kill people.
Nastiest fact: Snake fangs are folded inside their
                            mouths and pop out at the moment of
                            biting. Each fang is like a hollow needle
                            for injecting poison. Snakes strike at 2.4
                            metres a second – so the victim has just
                            0.25 of a second to dodge the fatal fangs!

SINISTER SNAKES

NAME: King Cobra

DESCRIPTION: Up to 5.5 metres long.

LIVES: India, southern China and Southeast Asia.

FIERCE FEATURES: Has a sinister pattern of two eyes and a nose on the hood behind its head. It displays this when it's angry or scared.

HORRIBLE HABITS: Eats other snakes. (Come to think of it, this habit could be quite useful.)

THE BAD NEWS: Its poison is strong enough to kill an elephant. So we humans don't stand a chance.

NAME: Okinawa Habu

DESCRIPTION: Up to 2 metres. Slender body with blotchy yellow ringed markings.

LIVES: Okinawa and neighbouring islands, Pacific Ocean. (Fortunately, it doesn't live anywhere else.)

FIERCE FEATURES: Heat-detectors on its head help it to find warm living flesh.

HORRIBLE HABITS: Enjoys snaking into peoples houses through tiny crevices.

THE BAD NEWS: Enjoys biting people.

THE VERY BAD NEWS: It's deadly poisonous.

NAME: Black Mamba

DESCRIPTION: 3-4 metres long. It's the largest venomous snake in Africa.

LIVES: Africa – south of the Sahara Desert.

FIERCE FEATURES: It can slither as fast as you can run.

HORRIBLE HABITS: It can swallow a whole rat and digest it in 9 hours. Most snakes take more than 24 hours.

BET YOU NEVER KNEW!
In 1906 crack-pot Colonel Richard Meinhertzhagen decided to test the black mamba's speed. He and his servants threw lumps of earth at an unfortunate snake. The enraged snake chased a volunteer whilst the Colonel carefully timed its speed. The snake had reached 11.2 km an hour (7 mph) when disaster struck. The man fell over! So the crack-shot colonel shot the snake.

Strangely enough, some people like snakes. Indeed, it's an astounding fact that some people even keep snakes as pets! Hopefully, your teacher isn't one of them. Or you might hear facts like these...

FIVE REASONS WHY SNAKES ARE CUDDLY[1]

1 Snakes are more scared of people than people are of snakes. After all, we're bigger than them.

1 OK, let's just say "not quite so nasty".

2 Snakes only bite people if the snake thinks it's being attacked. An Indian tradition says you should stop to chat to a poisonous Russell's viper. That way the snake won't bite you. Talking doesn't help because snakes are deaf (though they can feel sound vibrations passing through the ground). But standing still calms the snake down and could save your life.

3 Snakes are useful. Venom from the Russell's viper is made into a medicine that helps blood clot. Malaysian pit viper venom stops blood from clotting and this could be used to prevent unwanted blood clots inside the body.

4 Many nasty snake stories aren't true. For example, the Malaysian pit viper is nicknamed the 'hundred pacer' because that's how far people run after being bitten. Then they die. Not true. Victims get at least ten times that distance.

5 Humans kill far more snakes than snakes kill humans. For example, snake blood is used in traditional Chinese medicines. It's said to be very good for your liver and lungs. But not so good for thousands of wretched snakes.

So, fancy a cuddle? Thought not. But if you really find snakes charming why not become a snake charmer? Here's how to…

CHARM A SNAKE

1 Catch a venomous snake. A king cobra will do.
2 Remove its venom. Then if things go wrong you won't suffer a fatal bite. This technique is called 'milking' the snake. Grasp the snake by the back of its head and make it bite through a piece of paper stuck over a jar. Gently squeeze the poison glands

on either side of your snake's head so the lovely venom squirts out. (Don't worry about the snake – it can always make more venom.)

3 Put the snake in a basket and start playing your flute. After a while the snake will stick its head out to take a look.

4 Keep moving your flute about. The snake can't hear the music but it will follow your movements.

5 Beware – it's deciding when to strike!

6 If you get bitten whilst charming a snake and you forgot step **2** it's a good idea to know some first aid. So here's some useless advice.

Warning: Almost all these remedies are about as useful as a chocolate hot water bottle. Don't try these at home.

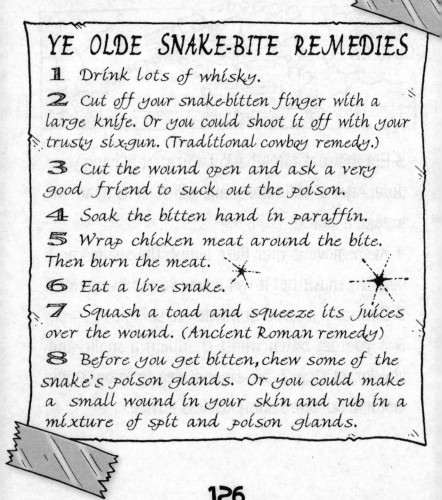

YE OLDE SNAKE-BITE REMEDIES

1 Drink lots of whisky.

2 Cut off your snake-bitten finger with a large knife. Or you could shoot it off with your trusty six-gun. (Traditional cowboy remedy.)

3 Cut the wound open and ask a very good friend to suck out the poison.

4 Soak the bitten hand in paraffin.

5 Wrap chicken meat around the bite. Then burn the meat.

6 Eat a live snake.

7 Squash a toad and squeeze its juices over the wound. (Ancient Roman remedy)

8 Before you get bitten, chew some of the snake's poison glands. Or you could make a small wound in your skin and rub in a mixture of spit and poison glands.

NOTES

1 This remedy was popular amongst US soldiers in the 1860s. It was even popular with soldiers who hadn't been bitten. In fact, the combined effects of the poison and whisky would probably kill the victim.

2 Useless. By the time the cowboy pulled the trigger the poison would have spread to the rest of his body.

3 This is dangerous because the venom could poison your friend, too.

4 Useless

5 Utterly useless – especially for the chicken.

6 Useless and cruel. Snakes have feelings, too.

7 Equally cruel and useless.

8 Yes – these do work. They're used by the Kung, San and Zulu peoples of Southern Africa. Anyone for a free trial?

SENSIBLE SNAKE ADVICE

By the way, if someone does get bitten (and there's more chance of winning the lottery) they should remember what the snake looked like. Snake bites are treated with a chemical called an antivenin (also known as anitvenom). This is a chemical produced naturally by the body in a bid to neutralize the poison. Getting extra amounts injected helps the body to recover more quickly. But the doctors need to know which antivenin to use. The bite victim should keep very still and send someone for help.

OK – so, snake-watching just isn't your favourite pastime. Perhaps a seaside holiday is your idea of fun instead. But just when you thought it was safe to go into the water…

NAUTICAL NASTIES

The most venomous snakes of all aren't on land. They're in the seas around India and East Asia. Sea snake venom is amongst the deadliest you can get. That's the bad news. The good news is sea snakes don't enjoy biting humans. So Indian fishermen often pull the wriggling snakes from their nets using only their bare hands. Is that brave – or what?

Another nautical nasty is the blue-ringed octopus. Yes – the sinister suckers have a poisonous bite. Scientists aren't sure exactly how poisonous the bite is because no one has volunteered to be bitten. Any takers? It's all in the cause of science.

Meanwhile, on land things aren't much better. Besides snakes there's a host of other...

PESKY POISONERS

1 The gila monster has a nasty method of poisoning its prey. This 50-cm-long lizard from the southern USA bites its victim. Then it chews the poison into the wound. Ouch!

2 Hot dry regions of the world are home to scorpions. Yes – they like it tough. A scorpion can live without water for three months and live without food for a year. And if it turns chilly – no problem. A scorpion will come back to life after being frozen for a few hours in a lump of ice. (This could be a problem if you tried to make scorpion-flavoured ice cream.)

3 Scorpions are active at night and hide during the day. Unfortunately, deadly scorpions such as the Trinidad scorpion love to snuggle down in a nice warm shoe. Next morning the shoe's owner gets a nasty surprise. That would really get your day off on the wrong foot.

SPOT THE WOMAN WALKING TO WORK
WITH A SCORPION IN HER SHOE

4 Water shrews are rat-like little beasts. They have poisonous spit that paralyses the frogs and fish they eat. That way the prey won't try to wriggle free whilst it's being scoffed by the shrew.

5 You've heard of dog eat dog? Well, dog eat toad isn't a very sensible idea either. The toad's warty skin contains glands that make a poison strong enough to kill a dog.

6 Remember the mixed-up duck-billed platypus? Just to confuse you further, the male platypus has poisonous spurs on its ankles. No one knows if the spurs are for fighting off other animals or for stabbing other males in fights over females. I expect they get used on the spur of the moment.

So how do you feel about poisonous creatures now? Worried, anxious, insecure? Join the club. That's what it's like to be a small animal when hungry hunters are on the prowl. Yep – it can be murder out there.

NARROW SQUEAKS

One moment you're nibbling a tasty morsel of smelly cheese. The next, you're running for your life with a hungry monster snapping at your tail. (By the way, the monster's name is Tiddles the cat.) Yes, if you're a mouse, life is full of narrow squeaks.

Yet, amazingly, many creatures manage to get away or even turn the tables on their attackers. Here's how they do it…

Some animals have their very own suits of armour. Could you do with this kind of protection?

NASTY NATURE GUIDE TO SELF DEFENCE

SAFETY FIRST

Stylish armour as worn by the three-banded armadillo of South America. Simply roll in a ball. If you fancy a bit of fun leave a chink in your armour. The attacker will insert a paw into the gap. Then shut the gap like a steel trap. Wham – Crunch – Ouch!

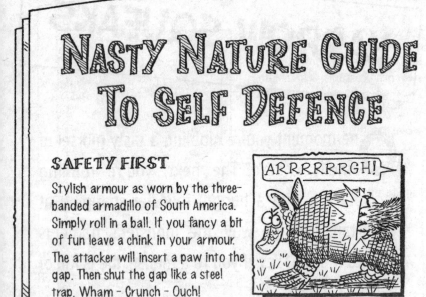

ARRRRRRGH!

TEACH YOUR ENEMIES A SHARP LESSON

Absolutely foolproof hedgehog and porcupine spiny armour. Choice of defence modes.

OUCH!

Hedgehog: Roll your body in a ball or ram your spines up an attacker's nose. Five thousand spines guaranteed in every hedgehog outfit. *Manufacturer's Warning: Never roll yourself in a ball in front of oncoming lorries. You'll feel a bit flat afterwards.*

HOWL!

Porcupine: Jab your barbed spines into an attacker's body. They won't get them out until their dying day. (That'll be quite soon afterwards.)

FANCY A SWIM?

Don't forget your porcupine fish swimming costume. Just inflate your swimsuit with water and stick your spines out. Gives sharks a real mouthful.

BE A HERO

With this discreet hero shrew outfit a specially strengthened backbone helps you feel tough inside. Guaranteed – if you're the size of a shrew a fully-grown human can stand on your back and you'll survive.*

NO PROBLEM!

*WARNING
DON'T DO THIS TO YOUR PET HAMSTER. ONLY HERO SHREWS HAVE THIS PROTECTION. OTHER FURRY ANIMALS GET SQUISHED

I'M OUT OF HERE!

NO ARMOUR?

So you can't find a suitable suit of armour? No problem. If an attacker gets too close simply kick up a stink. Take some advice from a skunk. If you want to get rid of an attacker try spraying them with foul juices. See next page for details . . .

SKUNK DEFENCE MANUAL

To be carried by all skunks at all times. You never know when you might need it.

1. Always give your attacker a warning. It's only fair to perform this little dance. Try practising it now.

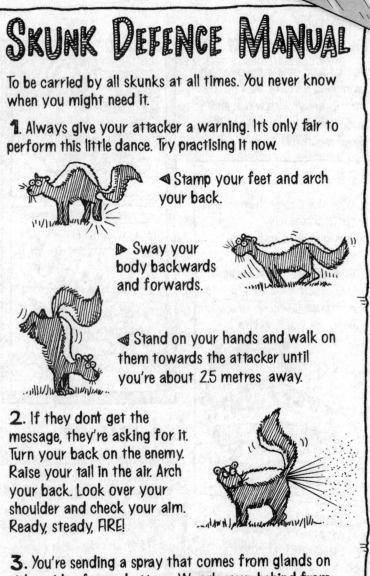

◀ Stamp your feet and arch your back.

▶ Sway your body backwards and forwards.

◀ Stand on your hands and walk on them towards the attacker until you're about 2.5 metres away.

2. If they don't get the message, they're asking for it. Turn your back on the enemy. Raise your tail in the air. Arch your back. Look over your shoulder and check your aim. Ready, steady, FIRE!

3. You're sending a spray that comes from glands on either side of your bottom. Waggle your behind from side-to-side so your enemy gets a good drenching.

NOTES

1 The spray contains a group of chemicals called thiols (thi-ols) and together they're reckoned to be the WORST SMELL IN THE WORLD. You can smell skunk juice at least 1.6 km away and it stays smelly for over a year.

2 The stink is so horrible that it damages the inside of the nose.

3 The juices taste so disgusting they make the victim throw up.

4 If the spray gets in the victim's eyes it causes temporary blindness.

5 But it doesn't bother the skunks a bit. The victim shouldn't complain too loudly either, for at least skunk spray isn't poisonous enough to kill. Some animals have really deadly poisonous defences.

POISONOUS PREY

Sitting on a tin-tack is a mere pin prick. Getting stung by a bee is a sore subject. Jumping in a bed of nettles – that's a little rash. All these things hurt but they're not really painful. Nothing like a brush with these creatures…

The stonefish uses its poisonous spines in self-defence. The fish lurks in shallow waters around the Australian coast and looks just like a stone (surprise, surprise) buried in the mud. But its poison causes

THE WORST PAIN IN THE WORLD. Humans who accidentally tread on the spines writhe in agony. Fortunately there's an antidote that can save the victim's life.

Don't spit at a spitting cobra. This 2-metre-long snake is likely to spit back a double jet of fluid from up to 2.5 metres. Just one gram is enough to kill 165 humans or 160,000 mice. As luck would have it the vicious venom won't kill you unless its injected into your blood but if gets in your eyes it can cause blindness. And your eyeballs are the sinister snake's number one target!

In the South American rainforest you'll see happy little frogs hopping about in the trees. "Why are they so brightly coloured?" you wonder. "Perhaps they will want to make friends." No way – they're warning you that they're deadly poisonous. Just 1 gram of the poison produced in their skin is enough to kill 100,000 people. Mind you, that doesn't save some frogs from an even worse torture. Some tribes grill the frogs over a fire and tip their arrows with the frog's deadly sweated juices.

WE'D BETTER HOP IT

ON THE RUN

If you don't have your own poison, you might try running away. Speedy animals such as antelopes can often out-run a hunter, especially if they've got a head start. The pronghorn – a creature like an antelope from western USA, reaches speeds of 98 km per hour (61 mph); horses and ostriches can gallop at 65 km per hour (40 mph). But how does that compare to us? Well – humans are left gasping. The fastest runners can only run at 36 km per hour (22.5 mph) for short distances. Then they run out of puff.

HURRY UP!

UNDER COVER

If you don't like running, you could stay still and blend in with the scenery. The sloth hangs out in the South American rainforest and moves at a stately 241 metres an hour (0.15 mph). It's so slow-moving that tiny green plants grow on its coat and this colouring makes it hard to spot amongst the trees. The word 'sloth' means lazy, and naturalist Charles Waterton objected to the sloth's laid back lifestyle...

The sloth is ... totally unfit to enjoy the blessings which have been so bountifully given to bountiful nature.

So what's wrong with doing no work and hanging around upside down in trees?

Many creatures hide successfully because they're the same colour as their surroundings. This trick is called 'camouflage'. But the real camouflage experts are creatures that change colour to match their surroundings. Take the flounder, for example – that's a type of flat-fish. A scientist once put a chess board on the bottom of a flounder's tank and within minutes the fish was a tasteful check pattern. Small colour grains in the flounder's skin move together or apart in response to signals from its brain. And this colourful trick leaves an attacker … floundering.

*PLAICE AND FLOUNDERS BELONG TO THE SAME FAMILY

If you can't change colour, you could try being invisible. Amazingly, some creatures such as the glass cat-fish have see-through bodies. They blend into the background because you can see it through their bodies. Yuck – imagine if you could see your school dinner after you'd eaten it.

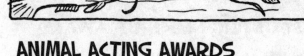

ANIMAL ACTING AWARDS

If all else fails you could pretend to be another more dangerous creature. Preferably something fierce and poisonous or something you wouldn't want to eat. Yes – animals can be actors, too. Welcome to the Animal Oscars.

BEST ACTOR /ACTRESS (Snake Category)

RUNNER-UP

The totally harmless king snake almost won for its superb impression of a poisonous coral snake. The king snake has the same red, yellow and black bands on its body but in a different order. So look carefully!

WINNER

The gopher snake wins for an outstanding performance as a rattlesnake. The gopher snake is harmless but hisses like a rattlesnake and even shakes its tail against dry leaves to rattle an attacker's nerves.

MOST DISGUSTING MAKE-UP AWARD

RUNNER-UP

The Budgett's frog from Argentina comes second in this category. It can swell up like a big ball of slime and then scream and grunt if you get too close.

WINNER

Our prize winner is the Ecuador tree frog. It sprawls on a leaf and looks just like a disgusting slimy bird dropping.

BEST ACTOR /ACTRESS (Plant Impression Category)

RUNNER-UP

The tawny frogmouth bird of Australia gives a terrific performance when it's asleep! It always sleeps on a tree branch and looks just like a rotten old twig.

WINNER

The leafy seadragon is a seahorse. It wins this award because it looks just like a disgusting rubbery bit of seaweed.

145

STRANGE SURVIVAL STRATEGIES

Animals have plenty more survival tricks and some of them are really strange. Which of these survival strategies is too strange to be true?

1 The horned lizard from the western parts of North America squirts blood from its eyes to frighten an attacker. TRUE/FALSE

2 The mimicking macaw of South America warns off attackers with a brilliant impression of an eagle's screech. TRUE/FALSE

3 Pallas's glass snake is actually a legless lizard. (That doesn't mean it's drunk.) When attacked the lizard's 1.5-metre body breaks into wriggling bits. In the confusion the lizard's head end manages to escape. It then grows a new body. TRUE/FALSE

Answers
1 TRUE 2 FALSE 3 TRUE

BITING BACK

Some creatures fight back if their friends are around to give them support. This is surprisingly common and the aim is always to frighten a hunter away. Birds, for example, will attack an owl if there's enough of them around. Chimps will gang up on a leopard and ground squirrels kick sand in a snake's face. Would you dare do this to your local bully?

When an animal is cornered without hope of escape it will often fight for its life. Even mice and their babies do this. So if someone says you're as "brave as a mouse" it's quite a compliment.

147

And so you reach the end of the day. A day spent dodging horrible hunters and fighting for your life. You're still alive ... just. Well, congratulations – you must be feeling peckish enough to eat – well, just about anything. I hope so. Now it's time for some gruesome gluttonish guzzling.

GRUESOME GUZZLING

Animals love eating and they always want second helpings. And what's more they don't care about good table manners. Burp! Oh, dear. Look what's coming to dinner...

WARNING

Anyone who is disgusted by guzzling and chomping and slurping should turn to the next chapter. Also, try to avoid reading this chapter aloud at the dinner table. You may find yourself the only person left and then you'll have to scoff everyone's food. Tragic!

INCREDIBLE EATING EQUIPMENT

Every animal has evolved jaws and mouth-parts that are perfectly suited to eating its favourite food. Here are a few examples...

1 Giraffes have tongues 30 cm long. Ideal for grasping leaves and yanking them off tall trees. But that's nothing – the South American anteater uses its sticky 60-cm tongue to lick up ants. It can manage as many as 30,000 a day.

2 The Asian and European hamster has floppy cheek pouches to store seeds. It sometimes stuffs these pouches so full that it can scarcely stagger home. These 'cheeky' hamsters store as much as 90 kg of seeds in their burrows.

3 Crocodiles have huge jaws useful for dragging their prey to a watery grave. A one-tonne crocodile has 13 tonnes worth of crushing power in its jaws. That's 26 times stronger than a human bite.

4 Elephants suck up water with their trunks and then blow it into their mouths. A thirsty jumbo can gulp down 14 litres at a time and drink 200 litres in a day.

5 Snake jaws unhinge to allow them to swallow prey that are bigger than their own heads. The African egg-eating snake uses this trick to swallow eggs without breaking them – and they're not even hard-boiled. Don't try this at home.

6 If you're a flamingo you eat by turning your head upside down underwater whilst balancing on your long legs. Tricky. Next you sweep your head from side to side and fill your mouth with water. Then use your tongue and a built-in sieve inside your mouth to suck out little wriggling water creatures. Tasty!

7 Chameleons sit around in trees waiting for insects

to drop by. Suddenly, a fly buzzes around and the chameleon yawns. Its long sticky tongue shoots out and back before you can see what's happened. The chameleon looks happy – if that's possible – and the fly? It's nowhere to be seen. Frogs and toads feed in the same revolting fashion.

TOP TOOL TRICKS

If your eating equipment lets you down you could always use tools to help you eat…

1 Green jays in the USA hold twigs in their beaks to poke under loose bark to dislodge stray insects.

2 Chimpanzees poke twigs into termite nests and lick the fat, wriggling insects off the twig.

3 A sea otter breaks open mussels on a stone balanced on its chest as it swims backstroke. (Don't try this in your local pool.)

4 Thrushes break open snail shells by banging the molluscs on a stone. You'll find the stones surrounded by broken snail shells.

Apart from the objects they use to help them eat, some animals have…

TERRIBLE TABLE MANNERS

1 A toad or frog uses its eyeballs to help it swallow a huge juicy fly. It blinks as it swallows, pushing the eyeballs backwards into its head forcing the fly down its throat. This makes swallowing easier, even if it looks disgusting. Gulp!

2 The red-billed quela is a small bird that lives in Africa, south of the Sahara desert. Its favourite food is seeds from farmer's crops. Nothing wrong with that, except that the quela likes to fly around in gangs of up to ten million strong. Once that lot have dropped in for dinner there's nothing left for anyone else.

3 Many animals hide spare food. We've all heard of squirrels burying nuts in the autumn, but do you know why dogs bury bones? When they lived in the wild thousands of years ago, dogs buried bones to stop other creatures guzzling the bone marrow. And they're still up to this old trick after all these years. Well – you can't teach an old dog new tricks.

4 The bearded vulture is wild about bone marrow, too. The villainous vulture drops bones from a dizzy height of 80 metres on to rocks until they break open. It has been rumoured to do this to unfortunate tortoises as well and even to enjoy dive-bombing mountaineers.

5 Owls eat small animals whole and then sick up the fur and bones in the form of pellets.

6 Starfish have a stomach-turning method of feeding on rotting fish and other prey. At the vital moment, the starfish squeezes its muscles until its stomach pops out of its mouth. The stomach's digestive juices dissolve the mouldering meal.

7 Many grass-eating animals, such as cows, have a special area of their stomach called the rumen. Here the food is softened for a few hours with stomach juices before being sicked up to the mouth for an extra chew. 'Chewing the cud' as it's called, helps to break down the tough plant material so it's easier to digest. Imagine if humans did this. It's certainly something to chew over.

FUNDAMENTAL FOOD FACTS

A food chain is nothing to do with clanking chains or dungeons. It's far more fascinating. 'Food chain' is a name used by naturalists to describe the vital links between animals and the unfortunate creatures they guzzle. Most food chains start with plants and a typical food chain goes something like this:

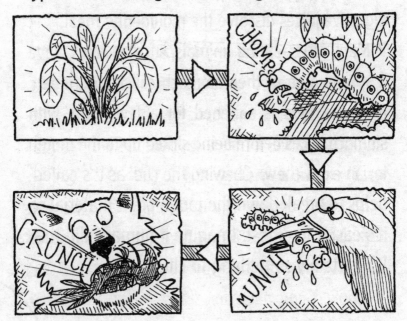

A food web (nothing to do with spiders) links the food chains in a particular habitat. So you might end up with something like this:

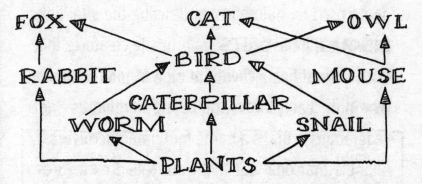

Animals depend on each other and on plants. Take away the plants, and the bugs and rabbits and mice starve. If they disappear the animals that eat them will go hungry, too.

Strangely enough if the top animals in the web disappear there can be nasty results, too. If the fox died out more rabbits would survive to breed and multiply. Good news for rabbits? Not necessarily. The rampaging rabbits guzzle plants. This is bad news for the bugs, birds, mice and other animals that depend on plants for food and shelter. And of course, the rabbits end up starving, too.

DISGUSTING DIETS

Each animal has a favourite type of food. Animals that only eat plants are called herbivores (not vegetarians – that's a name for human herbivores). Animals that only eat meat are called carnivores. And creatures that eat both (including humans who enjoy meat and two veg) are called omnivores. Simple, isn't it? But some animals also scoff sickening side dishes. Could you match the animal to the horrible things it eats?

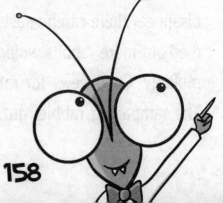

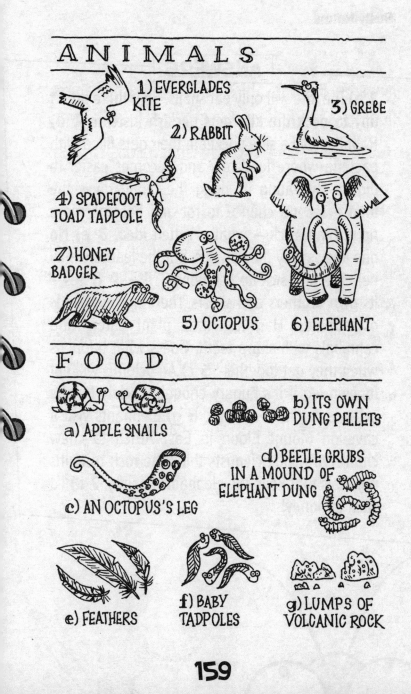

ANIMALS

1) EVERGLADES KITE

2) RABBIT

3) GREBE

4) SPADEFOOT TOAD TADPOLE

7) HONEY BADGER

5) OCTOPUS

6) ELEPHANT

FOOD

a) APPLE SNAILS

b) ITS OWN DUNG PELLETS

c) AN OCTOPUS'S LEG

d) BEETLE GRUBS IN A MOUND OF ELEPHANT DUNG

e) FEATHERS

f) BABY TADPOLES

g) LUMPS OF VOLCANIC ROCK

ANSWERS

1 a) The kite will only eat snails. So if there aren't any to peck the kite gets peckish instead. **2 b)** Rabbits have a side pocket in their guts filled with bacteria where food rots and becomes easier to digest. By eating its dung the rabbit gives the food a second chance to rot and become more nourishing. Yuck – what a rotten idea. **3 e)** No one knows why they do this, but the feathers may help the bird sick up fish bones. Nice. **4 f)** Yes – its own brothers and sisters. There are two kinds of tadpoles. Harmless little plant eaters and cannibals with sharp teeth. Guess what happens when they get together? **5 c)** An octopus will eat its own leg if it's hungry enough. Luckily for the octopus, it grows another. **6 g)** Elephants visit a cave on Mount Elgon in East Africa to chew chunks of rock. Scientists think the rock contains minerals that keep the elephants healthy. **7 d)** I'd stick to honey!

THE WORLD'S FUSSIEST EATER

Ever had to feed a really fussy pet? This will put your problems in perspective. Cape sugarbirds from South Africa only eat insects that live on the protea shrub. This is a rare plant only found at the southern tip of Africa. This feathered fusspot will also only drink protea nectar. Each bird has its own personal shrubs which it guards jealously from other sugarbirds.

THE WORLD'S LEAST FUSSY EATER

Like many other birds, ostriches swallow pebbles to help them grind up food in a special part of their stomachs called the gizzard.

Ostriches normally eat leaves and seeds but according to its owner, one bird ate…

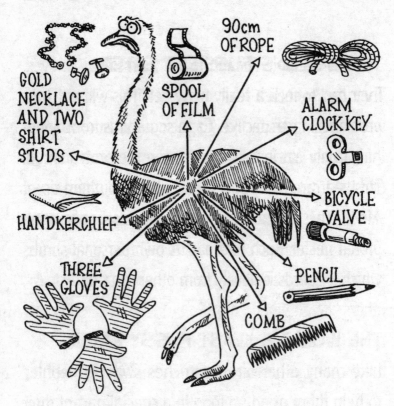

GOLD NECKLACE AND TWO SHIRT STUDS

SPOOL OF FILM

90cm OF ROPE

ALARM CLOCK KEY

HANDKERCHIEF

BICYCLE VALVE

THREE GLOVES

PENCIL

COMB

CLEAN CREATURES

Dirty animals? Filthy beasts? Don't you believe it! Despite their messy eating habits most animals like to get clean afterwards. But your parents might not approve if you copied some of their washing habits…

Cats are supple enough to lick themselves all over. They can even lick their own bottoms – wow! They wash their faces by licking their paws and rubbing their faces. Waste fur sticks to a cat's rough tongue and the front teeth strain out any bits of dirt and dead skin. They sick up any fur they swallow. Like any animal spit, cat spit is good for killing germs in the fur.

African warthogs, hippos, buffaloes and many others like nothing better than a refreshing roll in the mud. It's a sensible thing to do. The thick mud keeps them cool and protects their skin from biting insects.

Birds often clean themselves by allowing ants to crawl all over their bodies. They enjoy the delightful tingling sensation and the formic acid squirted by the ants kills nasty little parasites that get up their feathers. Sitting on top of a really smoky chimney does the same job. The smoke bumps off the pesky parasites.

NASTY SCAVENGERS

When an animal has eaten its fill, washed itself, and moved on – a new crowd of creatures comes to feast on the leftovers. The scavengers. A scavenger is a creature that eats food scraps and dead animals. It sounds nasty – but if somebody didn't eat the bones we'd be knee-deep in skeletons by now. So maybe scavengers don't deserve their nasty reputation? Read on, if you dare, and decide for yourself.

SCARY SCAVENGERS

1 Hagfish (also known as slimefish) look like swimming sausages with no jaws and no bones. They enjoy eating dead fish from the inside out – leaving just the skin and bones.

2 Komodo dragons are huge – they're the largest lizards in the world. These 3-metre long creatures skulk on the Indonesian island of Komodo. Despite their fearsome appearance, they mainly sniff out revolting rotting dead deer and pigs for their tea.

3 At Harar in Ethiopia until the late 1960s hyenas were used to keep the streets clean of waste meat from butcher's stalls. Each year the hard-working hyenas were rewarded with a lovely smelly dead cow. The hyenas did a good job but they had an embarrassing habit of digging up dead bodies.

4 While we are on this grisly subject, our old friend the snapping turtle (last seen lurking in the sewers) enjoys scoffing unwanted bodies. So keen is the turtle that the police in Florida, USA use tame snapping turtles to sniff out corpses. Imagine what the turtles might get as a treat! And talking about dead bodies…

Nasty nature fact file

Name:	Vultures
The basic facts:	Vultures spend most of their time gliding about looking for a carcass to scoff. Hungry vultures fight over a carcass and gorge themselves until they can scarcely fly.
Nastiest fact:	Vultures have bald heads because feathers would get clotted with gore when they stick their heads into carcasses. Erk!

So would you want to invite a vulture to dinner? Some people would – here's their story.

VULTURE RESTAURANTS

In the 1970s, South Africa's Cape vulture was in trouble. Much of the area around their nests had been turned into farmland. There were few dead animals for them to eat. Worse still, the vultures were feeding their young on junk food. No – that's not hamburgers but real junk food – such as ring pulls from drink cans. This diet did nasty things to the vulture chicks' insides. Small wonder half the chicks were dying every year.

167

That's where the vulture restaurants came in. The plan was simple, but brilliant. Fence off an area of land and leave a few carcasses lying around. Make sure you remember to break the bones so the vultures can guzzle the tasty bone marrow. So while some people scoffed at the idea, the vultures scoffed some delicious dead animals.

Today there are more than 100 vulture restaurants offering exciting and varied menus of dead racehorses, bulls and the odd elephant.

And once there was even a human on the menu. Devoted vulture-lover Mickey Lindbergh shot himself in 1987 at a vulture restaurant. His last act on Earth was to make sure his beloved vultures got fed. On his own dead body!

But there's one creature that makes vultures look like innocent little doves. A creature that makes the worst teacher seem tame and rather fluffy. The vile, violent, villainous, verminous, vicious, voracious RAT! Just look what this creature can do:

THE ADVENTURES OF SUPER RAT

A rat can fall from a five-storey building and land on its feet – unharmed.

It can squeeze through a hole the size of a fifty pence coin.

Fight creatures three times its size … and win!

A rat can survive being flushed down a toilet. In fact, this could be a new rat water sport.

In 2005, Razza the runway rat escaped from a New Zealand island and swam 400 metres to another one.

Rats will happily eat soap and drink beer. And scoff anything else remotely edible – including school dinners.

But despite its gross eating habits, a rat can taste tiny amounts of poison in its food. Yes – even if the poison is only one millionth of the food's weight.

HE'S EATING IT . . . WAIT A MOMENT . . . FANTASTIC!

Rats can gnaw through anything including lead pipes, wood, bricks, concrete and live electrical cables.

UNBELIEVABLE!

COR!

Rats use smelly pee to mark their way. They pee on each other and even pee near food to show other rats it's nice to eat. You might also like to know that a rat can't vomit or burp, even if it doesn't like its dinner.

One fifth of all human food crops are eaten by rats. In India alone the amount of grain eaten by rats would be enough to fill a train 4,800 km (3,000 miles) long.

In return for all this food, rat bites and rat fleas spread deadly diseases such as bubonic plague to humans.

LOVEABLE RATS?

Despite all this some people claim that rats aren't so bad. Do you believe them – or do you smell a rat? Here are some nicer rat facts to rattle around in your brain.

1 All this talk about 'dirty rats' is very unfair. Rats spend much of their lives licking themselves clean.

2 Rats don't eat humans – when they're alive. So if you're attacked by a rat you can frighten it off by screaming. Well, you would – wouldn't you? That way the rat knows you're still alive and able to fight back.

3 Rats make more affectionate pets than hamsters and guinea pigs. Rats enjoy being stroked and cuddled and tickled – but don't try this with wild rats.

4 If you get tired of your pet you could always eat it. Rats taste like rabbit and deep fried rat with coconut oil is a delicious traditional delicacy in the Philippines.

5 One pair of rats can have 70 little rats a year. And if they all produce young, you could end up with 1,500 rats at the end of the year. Despite this, rats really care for their families and only eat their babies when they're really hungry.

And compared with some animal lifestyles this really is happy families.

A BIT OF BREEDING

What's your family like? Close, friendly, loving? Or do they row a lot and throw things at one another? Many animals care about their young and look after them as best they can. (Tell that to your parents.) But some animal families aren't so happy and they have the nasty habit of eating one another. This gives a totally different meaning to the phrase 'family meal-times'.

BAFFLING BREEDING

First stage in setting up an animal family is to find a mate – that's a member of the opposite sex to start a family with. Male animals display a range of baffling behaviour to attract a suitable female.

Just as human teenagers dress up to go out in the evening, male birds 'dress up' to attract a mate. Many species grow brightly coloured feathers, such as the gorgeous peacock or the bottle-green head of a mallard drake.

Many male birds sing to attract attention and the females choose the loudest singer. But other animals also 'sing' to attract a mate. For example, humpback whales' songs can be heard hundreds of kilometres away – just in case there's a suitable mate in some distant corner of the ocean. Even American grasshopper mice get up on their haunches at mating time and sing squeaky little songs.

Another trick used by some male birds is to build the female a nice cosy nest to lay her eggs in. But no bird goes to the baffling lengths of the bowerbird of Australia.

BIRD-BRAIN ESTATE AGENTS

HELPING YOU TO FIND YOUR IDEAL NEST

FOR SALE
A beautiful bower

IN BRIEF...
The accommodation consists of a platform with straight walls made of woven plants.

FANTASTIC FEATURES
The bower comes complete with specially chosen designer contents: an interesting collection of blue coloured shells, feathers, bottle tops, pen tops, pegs, animal bones, bird skulls and bits of dead insects. The present owner has painted the walls a tasteful shade of blue using chewed-up blueberries, spit and a stick held in his bill.

Note: 1. Intending purchasers should bear in mind that the property needs repainting every day in any colour so long as it's blue. Also, the neighbouring bowerbirds often try to steal things from the nest.*

* 2. OK, so you don't like blue. Don't worry. Fawn-breasted bower-birds only use pale green objects and Lanterbach's bowerbird prefer grey and red. So you've a lovely choice of tasteful colour schemes for your nest.

Another method of finding a mate if you're a male animal is to fight off all the other males. This makes the females fancy you and even if they don't you're the only male around. So they don't have any choice.

Male animals that fight include deer (that's why stags grow antlers), cats and giraffes. The giraffes try to butt each other but it generally turns into a neck and neck contest. Male birds also fight. Like most fights between animals of the same species, it's rare for anyone to get killed. Only horrible humans kill their own kind in any numbers. But why then do robins sometimes meet messy ends?

BLOOD ON THE TRACKS

You probably know robins as cute birds that appear on Christmas cards. But have you heard that jolly little rhyme that sometimes gives young children bad dreams?

"Who killed Cock Robin?
I, said the sparrow,
With my bow and arrow,
I killed Cock Robin."

"What a nasty sparrow," you might say. "How cruel to kill such a cute robin." But was the sparrow's confession genuine? Read the notes and decide for yourself. Who do you think really killed Cock Robin? **a)** A female robin **b)** His own son **c)** A passing eagle.

THE CASE NOTES OF CHIEF
INSPECTOR BIRD

<u>Monday</u>

Cock Robin was found dead
with his legs sticking up in the
air at 6 am this morning. The
body had been

PARTLY PLUCKED

partly plucked. To
begin with, I suspected the
neighbour's cat. But she was in
bed at the time and the post-
mortem reveals the victim had
been pecked to death. I suspect

ORIGINAL SUSPECT

fowl play. I have offered a reward of 50 dead
worms for any information.

<u>Tuesday</u>

Cock Robin was last seen
fluffing out his red breast
and singing loudly in a bid
to chase away an
intruder. Then there was
silence. A sparrow has given

SPARROW CLAIMS HE DID IT

himself up and is singing like a canary – but I
don't believe his confession. The evidence all
points in another direction.

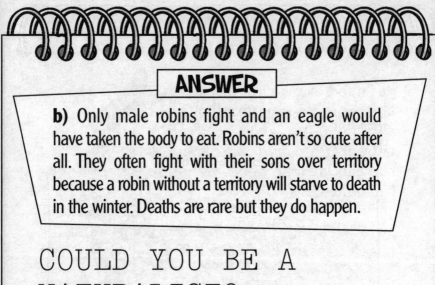

b) Only male robins fight and an eagle would have taken the body to eat. Robins aren't so cute after all. They often fight with their sons over territory because a robin without a territory will starve to death in the winter. Deaths are rare but they do happen.

COULD YOU BE A NATURALIST?

Most birds feed their young by regurgitating their meals down their chicks' throats. Regurgitation — that's the posh word for being sick or chucking up. Lovely. Dutch naturalist Nikolaas Tinbergen (1903–1988), tried to discover what triggers this. He noticed that herring gull chicks peck at a red blotch on their parents' beaks. So Tinbergen set out to discover how important this blotch was.

He made a very crude dummy gull's head complete with blotch. He also got hold of a dead gull's head and

painted out the blotch. Which did
the chicks prefer to peck at?
a) The dead gull's head — they
thought it was their supper.
b) The dummy head because it had the
blotch.
c) Neither — the sight of the dead
gull's head upset the chicks so much
they forgot to peck at anything.

ANSWER
b) What did you expect? Would the
sight of a human head make you feel
hungry? Tinbergen went on to prove
that the red colour wasn't
important. Any colour was OK as long
as the patch was clearly visible.

THE BLOTCH

THEY LOOK
UNHAPPY...

...PERHAPS
IT'S BECAUSE
THEY'VE HAD
THEIR HEADS
CUT OFF

BET YOU NEVER KNEW!

Some babies don't look like their parents and their appearance changes completely as they grow up.

1 Tadpoles don't look like adult frogs or toads. Tadpoles have tails and no legs, for example, and they have breathing gills outside their bodies. Gradually the gills are absorbed and suddenly a leg or two pops through the tadpole's body. For a while a tadpole might have two or three legs. After all four legs appear the tadpole's tail is absorbed into its body. Life for a frog can be horribly confusing.

2 A baby kangaroo looks like a little pink worm the size of a baked bean. It's only one twelve thousandth the size of its mum. Somehow it crawls through its mum's fur until it finds her pouch and there feeds off her milk. After seven months the baby kangaroo, or joey, is big enough to hop around outside the pouch. And after eleven months it has to leave the pouch for good. Almost immediately another baby takes its place.

3 In terms of growing that's nothing. A blue whale begins its life as an egg produced by its mum that weighs only 0.0009922 g. The baby blue whale grows to 26 tonnes. That's like you increasing your weight 30,000,000,000 (thirty billion) times.

GOOD PARENTS AWARDS

Many animal parents feed and lick their babies clean. And here are some especially good parents…

Third prize

Ma Croc

Crocodile mums bury their eggs in the sand by rivers. Three months later they hear the babies cheeping from inside their eggs and dig them up again. After the babies hatch, mum carries them in her massive jaws down the river and lets them go. For the next few months she feeds them on choice

183

morsels such as juicy frogs, bits of fish and the occasional crunchy insect.

Second prize
Mrs Surinam Toad

She's really ugly – even by toad standards. (Even her friends would agree – if she had any.) She has no eyes, no teeth and no tongue and a huge mouth that eats anything that moves. Yet somehow she loads her tadpoles on to her back and encases them in bubbles under her skin. Then she patiently carries the tadpoles for two months until they emerge as ugly little versions of herself.

WE'RE GOING OUT TO PLAY FOR A BIT, MUM

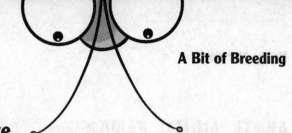

First prize

Mr Emperor Penguin

When Mrs Penguin goes down to the sea to hunt fish, Mr Penguin joins thousands of other males standing about in the freezing cold of Antarctica. Each male balances a single large egg on top of his feet to keep it warm. If the egg falls the chick inside will die. And there the male stands for 40 days and nights without food or shelter until his mate returns. Sometimes the temperatures drops to -40°C (-40°F) What a hero!

AWFUL ANIMAL FAMILIES

Of course, not all animal families are as caring as that. Many kinds of fish, reptiles and amphibians simply abandon their eggs and leave the young to survive on their own. If they can.

For fish especially, it doesn't matter if some youngsters get eaten. A single cod can lay six million eggs at a time. If all of them survived the seas would be crammed with cod. And that's what Darwin's idea of natural selection was about. Enough cod will live to breed the next generation.

Not all animals are looked after by both parents. Elephant families, for example, are made up of females under the command of the oldest female. She decides where they go and when they should go for water. The babies are looked after by all the females but when the males grow up they're chased away to live with other males. If you've got an awful brother you might think the elephants have the right idea. If you're a female yourself, that is.

LETHAL LESSONS

If you're a baby animal you need to learn some urgent lessons in survival. And if you're lucky your parents will teach you.

1 Guillemot chicks have to learn how to swim and fly. So their parents chuck them off a cliff. If they fly – good. If not, they'd better learn to swim.

2 Mother swallows take food to their chicks but hover just out of reach. If the chicks want to grab their grub they'd better learn to fly first.

3 Cheetah mums catch a gazelle, then release it for their cubs to chase. If the gazelle escapes the cubs get taught a lesson: they starve.

4 Eventually, when her cubs get too big, a grizzly bear mum chases them up a tree and wanders off. Now begins the biggest lesson of all: how to survive alone.

Every young animal (and human children, too) must learn one other lesson. At the end of the day they'll need to go to sleep. But while you're tucked up in your bed some creatures are on the prowl. And they're out to make a killing.

NOCTURNAL NASTIES

Night. A time of mystery and … danger. It's hard to see in the dark and things appear strange and sinister in the moonlight. There are sudden sounds – a scream or is it just a squawk? Something scuttles through the undergrowth. And in the shadows something dark and menacing is looking for its first meal of the night. Will you live to see the dawn?

Nocturnal (that means active by night) animals are adapted to living at night. Their bodies have evolved to suit their lifestyle in certain ways.

Take an African bushbaby, for example. This cute monkey-like creature lives in trees. It spends the night hunting insects, birds, fruit and anything else it can grab.

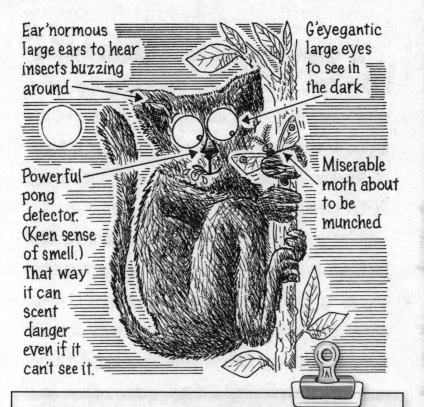

Ear'normous large ears to hear insects buzzing around

G'eyegantic large eyes to see in the dark

Powerful pong detector. (Keen sense of smell.) That way it can scent danger even if it can't see it.

Miserable moth about to be munched

BET YOU NEVER KNEW!

You might know that nocturnal animals go out at night and sleep during the day. But did you know that the posh scientific word for animals that go to sleep at night and are active during the day is diurnal (di-urn-al)? Animals that are most active at dawn and dusk are crepuscular (crep-us-cu-lar). Do you know any crepuscular people?

You might think that being nocturnal sounds rather tiring. But consider the advantages for a small animal. It's cool and moist at night – which is fine if you live in a hot, dry country. There are lots of shadows to hide in and many of the larger, fiercer creatures are fast asleep.

Unfortunately, there are nocturnal hunters, too. Owls swoop out of the darkness to grab unsuspecting shrews in their grasping talons. Hyenas and lions prowl the African grasslands and bats screech through the skies. Have you ever seen bats flapping around in the evening? Creepy – aren't they? And you wouldn't want to get too close. But some naturalists are batty about bats. According to them bats are brilliant.

Here's why...

BRILLIANT BATS

1 Bats spend most of their lives hanging upside down from the ceiling. According to a bat scientist, that's an interesting way to live.

AND I SHOULD KNOW!

2 Baby bats are born upside down. Usually their mother catches them before they hit the ground and they cling to their mother's fur with their teeth. Could you imagine a human baby doing this?

3 You can't say "as blind as a bat" because bats aren't actually blind – although they can't see well. But then bats don't need eyes. As they fly, they make high-pitched sounds and listen for echoes bouncing off the body of a flying insect. By homing in on these echoes a bat can gobble up a nice juicy insect in mid-air.

4 A flying bat makes one call a second. The calls get faster and faster as the bat closes in to grab its victim.

BET YOU NEVER KNEW!

Carlsbad cavern, New Mexico, USA is alive with bats. Up to 20 million Mexican free-tailed bats go there each summer. The babies hanging from its walls are packed together 3,000 to a square metre. But somehow mother bats, returning from a night's hunting, find their own babies using hearing and smell. They recognize the babies in the crowd by their cries and the smell of their bodies. And naturalists have found that the bats are right 80 per cent of the time.

NASTY SLEEPING HABITS

Most animals don't bother to go out at night. They like nothing better than a good night's kip. Scientists think that sleep boosts an animal's brain and ability to fight disease. It also saves energy.

So taking a quiet snooze is more sensible than running around all night. Mind you, some creatures have nasty sleeping habits.

1 Chimps construct beds from springy branches. But they don't bother to make their beds in the morning. They simply throw them away together with any dirt and fleas. Don't you wish you could do this?

2 When parrot fish go to sleep they wrap themselves in a ball of slime with a small hole to breathe through. This keeps them safe from marauding eels.

3 Only birds and mammals dream. Fish, amphibia and reptiles don't.

4 The prize for the most uncomfortable sleeping position must go to the blue-crowned hanging parrot. This bird sleeps hanging upside down from a branch. Its green back looks like a leaf so there's less chance of being spotted by a hunter.

Some animals find it pays to be asleep most of the time. Take the Australian koala, for example.

A DAY IN THE LIFE OF A KOALA

The night
Clambered about in my tree.

Guzzled 1kg of eucalyptus leaves – this is the life. Yawn. Now for a bit of shut-eye – reckon I've earned it.

5.10am
Found a nice branch to curl up on. Zzzzzz.

7.30am
Some human woke me up! Can't they let a koala have a decent kip? They've slung a rope loop around my neck.

What cheek! Now they're trying to yank me off my tree – better dig my claws in.

NOTES: Koalas are most active at night. disguise of leaf taste eucalyp doesn't bues them at all.

NOTES: The ko diet of leaves nourishing. In fact, it sends them to sleep!

NOTES: When there are too many koalas in an area it's a good idea to move some before they eat all the eucalyptus leaves and starve. Not all koalas like their new homes, however. Some homesick koalas have made their slow way back to their favourite tree!

7.32am
Arggggh! They've caught me.
Lucky I've [got?]
sharp claw[s] and
teeth. [I'll?] teach
That [one a?] lesson.
the[m?]

Notes:
By sleeping in the hottest part of the day the koala avoids over-heating or even getting thirsty. It gets all the moisture it needs from juicy leaves.

[been?] moved in a crate. Oh
[wel]l - this tree looks OK.
[b]ack to sleep.

Notes:
The koala spends over 18 hours a day snoozing its cute little head off. Even when it's awake it usually moves slowly and its lifestyle makes the sloth look like a go-getter in a hurry.

5, 6, 7 pm
Zzzzz

-9pm
Yawn. What's for breakfast.
Eucalyptus leaves will do
just fine.

198

WINTER SLUMBERLAND

Many animals don't stop at sleeping the night away. Some sleep most of the winter and only get really active in the spring. This is called hibernation – but you probably know that already. So here are a few more details to keep you awake.

Hibernation is a good idea because animals need lots of food to keep warm in cold weather. But during the winter there is less food around. By sleeping much of the time an animal can survive without having to find this extra food. Some animals live off stored food in their burrows and others live off their own body fat – built up by guzzling as much as possible in the warmer months.

Animals that hibernate include tortoises, squirrels, dormice, bats and some snakes. During hibernation an animal's breathing and pulse slow down and its body temperature may drop by 50°C (112°F). It's in a very deep sleep and it can appear dead. This has led to early burials for many unfortunate tortoises.

Zzzzz.

POOR OLD FLASH, HE WAS A LOVELY TORTOISE

PITY I DON'T SNORE – AT LEAST THEY'D HAVE KNOWN I WAS STILL ALIVE

NASTY NATURE?

Some animals seem really nasty. They look repulsive and do nasty things to other animals. Some animals have horrible weapons or use nasty cunning tricks to catch their prey. Some eat really foul food. And their eating habits are enough to put you off your dinner.

BUT IT'S MY TURN TO PECK THE EYEBALLS OUT

But so what? You can't expect animals to be polite and kind to one another. These are qualities you might find in humans – if you're lucky. Animals have to be tough to survive in a tough world. For them it's more important to be alive than to be nice. For an animal, every day is a battle for life. Animals don't know when they wake up in the morning whether they'll see the day through, or end up as a tasty snack for a larger creature.

And for all their nasty habits, we humans find animals immensely useful. They provide the raw materials for our food, and horses and dogs work hard for us. Unlike some humans – animals are never boring. We laugh at them and enjoy their companionship. Of course, some animals are nasty but they're also beautiful, fascinating and splendid in their dazzling variety.

You can see why naturalists spend their entire lives studying animals in their natural habitats. And how they get horribly excited if they manage to photograph a rare creature from an unusual angle. Yep, there's no doubt – for us humans, animals have a nasty fascination. But that's Horrible Science for you!

. . . FASCINATING . . . IT'S MOST UNUSUAL FOR THIS TYPE OF SNAKE . . . THEY USUALLY EAT LIZARDS

HORRIBLE INDEX